CHINA

Harness ornaments,
7th–6th century B.C.

Sword and sheath,
decorated with brass
and tortoiseshell

Stucco head of
a Bodhisattva,
8th–9th century

Sihu, or spike
fiddle, and bow,
19th century

Carved
lacquer boxes

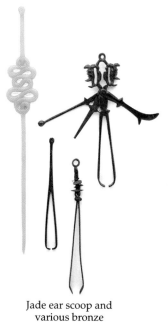

Jade ear scoop and
various bronze
tweezers

Modern
calligraphy brushes

EYEWITNESS GUIDES

CHINA

Written by
ARTHUR COTTERELL

Photographed by
ALAN HILLS & GEOFF BRIGHTLING

Pottery tomb
figures, 7th–8th
century

DORLING KINDERSLEY
London • New York • Stuttgart

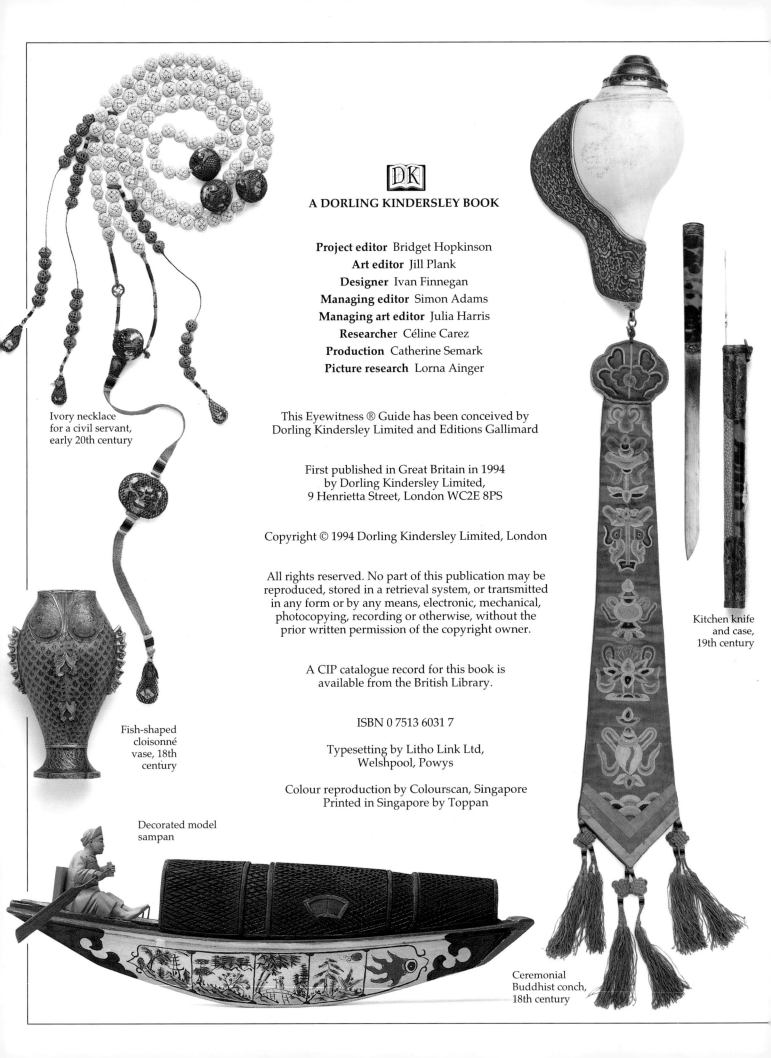

DK

A DORLING KINDERSLEY BOOK

Project editor Bridget Hopkinson
Art editor Jill Plank
Designer Ivan Finnegan
Managing editor Simon Adams
Managing art editor Julia Harris
Researcher Céline Carez
Production Catherine Semark
Picture research Lorna Ainger

This Eyewitness ® Guide has been conceived by
Dorling Kindersley Limited and Editions Gallimard

First published in Great Britain in 1994
by Dorling Kindersley Limited,
9 Henrietta Street, London WC2E 8PS

A CIP catalogue record for this book is
available from the British Library.

ISBN 0 7513 6031 7

Typesetting by Litho Link Ltd,
Welshpool, Powys

Colour reproduction by Colourscan, Singapore
Printed in Singapore by Toppan

Ivory necklace
for a civil servant,
early 20th century

Fish-shaped
cloisonné
vase, 18th
century

Decorated model
sampan

Kitchen knife
and case,
19th century

Ceremonial
Buddhist conch,
18th century

Contents

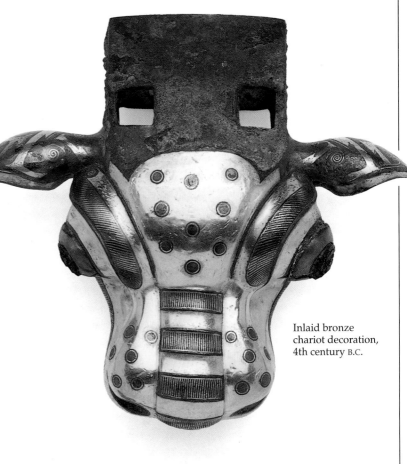

Inlaid bronze
chariot decoration,
4th century B.C.

The world's oldest empire

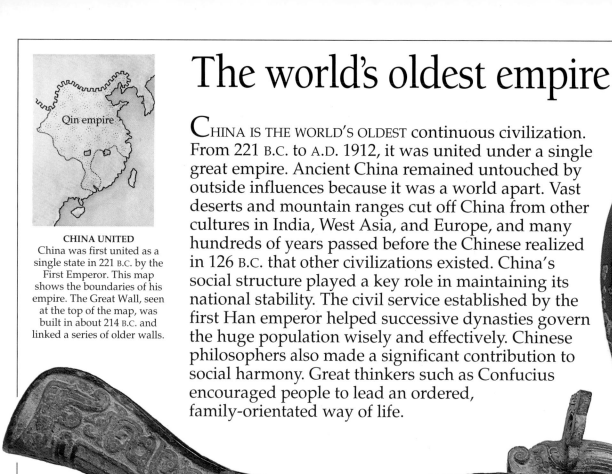

CHINA IS THE WORLD'S OLDEST continuous civilization. From 221 B.C. to A.D. 1912, it was united under a single great empire. Ancient China remained untouched by outside influences because it was a world apart. Vast deserts and mountain ranges cut off China from other cultures in India, West Asia, and Europe, and many hundreds of years passed before the Chinese realized in 126 B.C. that other civilizations existed. China's social structure played a key role in maintaining its national stability. The civil service established by the first Han emperor helped successive dynasties govern the huge population wisely and effectively. Chinese philosophers also made a significant contribution to social harmony. Great thinkers such as Confucius encouraged people to lead an ordered, family-orientated way of life.

CHINA UNITED
China was first united as a single state in 221 B.C. by the First Emperor. This map shows the boundaries of his empire. The Great Wall, seen at the top of the map, was built in about 214 B.C. and linked a series of older walls.

Qin empire

Bronze ritual water vessel, Zhou dynasty

Bronze ritual wine vessel, Shang dynasty

Bronze spearheads, Warring States period

Terracotta soldier, Qin dynasty

SHANG
China's first great dynasty was the Shang. This Bronze Age civilization is renowned for its skilful metalwork and for the emergence of the first Chinese writing. The Shang kings and their nobles ruled the mainly rural population from walled towns and cities. Horse-drawn chariots were the chief means of transport.

c. 1650–1027 B.C.

ZHOU
Confucius looked back on the early years of the Zhou dynasty as a golden age. The Zhou kings maintained the Shang practice of ancestor worship, and society was organized on a feudal system: great lords ruled the peasant farmers from large estates.

1027–256 B.C.

WARRING STATES PERIOD
As the Zhou declined, great lords fought each other for supremacy in what became known as the Warring States period. Vast armies clashed in large-scale battles and hundreds of thousands of men were killed. Confucius and other philosophers taught more peaceful ways of being, but their ideas were not adopted until later years.

481–221 B.C.

QIN
In 221 B.C. the First Emperor united China under the Qin dynasty. He built the Great Wall to protect his empire from the northern nomads, and standardized Chinese script, coins, weights, and measures. The First Emperor united China so firmly that afterwards the Chinese people regarded imperial rule as the only form of government.

221–207 B.C.

Bronze mirror,
Han dynasty

Carved stone Buddha,
Tang dynasty

Ceramic water vessel,
Period of disunity

Engraved silver dish,
Tang dynasty

HAN
The Han emperors consolidated the imperial system by establishing a national civil service that was to run China for the next 2,000 years. Educated officials studied the teachings of Confucius and were selected by a rigorous examination system. State factories manufactured all kinds of goods, from iron ploughshares to silk cloth.

207 B.C.–A.D. 220

PERIOD OF DISUNITY
In the Period of disunity, China was divided into separate states, although it was briefly united under the Western Jin dynasty (265–316). Foreign peoples overran northern China, and in the south, various dynasties struggled for power. The gentle ideas of Buddhism first became popular in these years of unrest.

221–589

SUI
The Sui dynasty reunified northern and southern China. In their brief reign, the Sui emperors rebuilt the Great Wall and dug the Grand Canal. This great waterway linked the Yangzi and Yellow rivers, which improved communications and enabled grain and soldiers to be transported around the empire.

589–618

TANG
Under the Tang emperors, the Chinese empire expanded to become a great world power. This was a time of prosperity and cultural renaissance in which both art and trade flourished. The civil service was reformed so that officials were recruited by merit rather than birth, and poetry was added to the examination syllabus.

618–906

Continued on next page

The empire continues

Although the Chinese empire experienced periods of unrest and disunity, and even conquests by foreign peoples, it existed as a strong state until modern times. China's borders ebbed and flowed with its changing dynasties, and the position of the imperial capital shifted several times, but the centralized government set up by the First Emperor survived for over 2,000 years. There were many great innovations and technological advances throughout the empire's long history. The inventions of gunpowder, paper, printing, and industrial machinery all had an effect on Chinese culture. Nevertheless, the customs and traditions of the Chinese people, particularly those of the rural population, stayed remarkably constant.

Kubilai Khan, the great Mongol ruler

Blue dish with a dragon motif, Song dynasty

Bronze flower vase, Song or Yuan dynasty

Blue and yellow glazed dish, Ming dynasty

Greenware dish, Yuan dynasty

FIVE DYNASTIES
In the Five Dynasties period, China was again briefly divided into north and south. A part of northern China fell under foreign rule, while the south was divided into numerous small states, many more than the name Five Dynasties implies. Southern China continued to prosper both culturally and economically.

907–960

SONG
China was united once more under the Song dynasty and reached its greatest heights of civilization. Advances in science and technology produced a minor industrial revolution, and the world's first mechanized industry was developed. Commodities such as iron and salt were produced on an industrial scale and were transported to distant parts of the empire on improved road and canal networks. The Song emperors were great patrons of the arts, and poetry, painting, and calligraphy reached new levels of perfection.

960–1279

YUAN
In the 13th century, China was conquered by the Mongols who established their own dynasty, the Yuan. Throughout Mongol rule, Chinese scholars were banned from the civil service and many of them retired to write literature. Because the Mongols controlled the entire length of the Silk Road, international trade thrived. Many merchants became rich by exporting Chinese luxury goods. Marco Polo, and later other Europeans, visited China and reported on the marvels of its civilization.

1279–1368

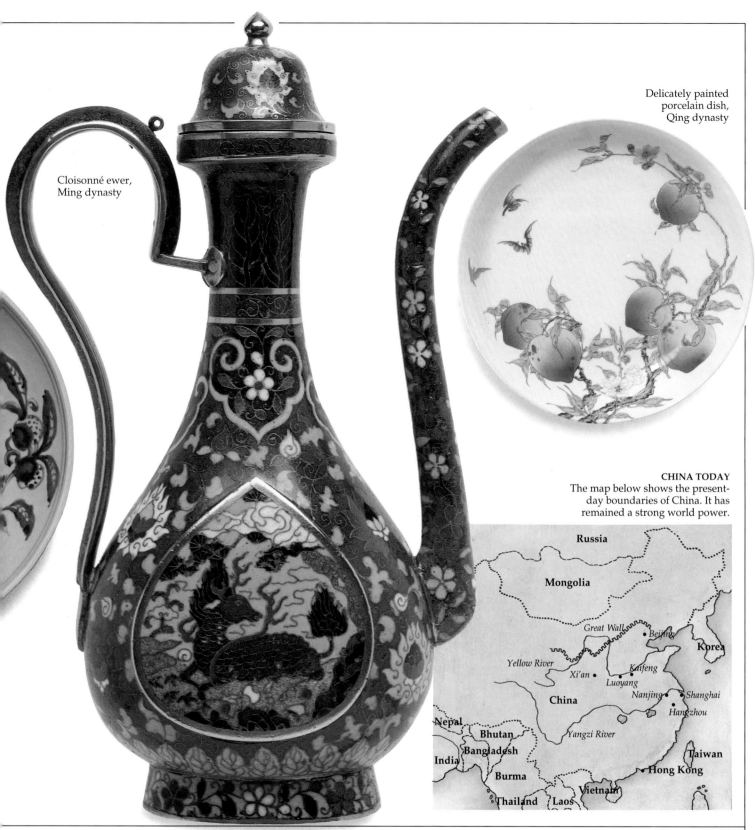

Cloisonné ewer,
Ming dynasty

Delicately painted
porcelain dish,
Qing dynasty

CHINA TODAY
The map below shows the present-day boundaries of China. It has remained a strong world power.

Russia

Mongolia

Great Wall

Beijing

Korea

Yellow River

Kaifeng

Xi'an

Luoyang

Nanjing

Shanghai

China

Hangzhou

Nepal

Bhutan

Yangzi River

India

Bangladesh

Taiwan

Burma

Hong Kong

Vietnam

Thailand

Laos

MING
After less than a hundred years, the Chinese drove the Mongols out of China and replaced them with the last Chinese dynasty, the Ming. The Ming emperors set up a new capital in Beijing, strengthened the Great Wall, and improved the Grand Canal. They also attempted to re-establish Chinese prestige by sending Admiral Zheng He on seven great maritime expeditions to visit foreign rulers. Chinese culture flourished once again, and the Ming dynasty became famous for its exquisite arts and crafts.

QING
The Chinese empire eventually collapsed under a foreign dynasty, the Manchu, or Qing dynasty. The Qing emperors lived in fear of a Chinese revolt and clung to outdated traditions. For the first time, Chinese technology fell behind other countries. Foreign powers began to demand trade concessions and, after a series of wars, China was forced to yield both concessions and territory. In 1911 the Chinese overthrew the weakened Qing government and formed a republic. The Last Emperor stepped down in 1912.

AFTER THE EMPIRE
The Chinese republic established in 1912 lasted for only 37 years. It was destroyed by war with Japan and, after the Second World War, civil conflict. In the civil war between 1946 to 1949, Communist forces were victorious. The Chinese Communist Party set up the present-day People's Republic of China in 1949.

1368–1644

1644–1912

1912– present

Jade axehead,
eastern China
c. 4500–2500 B.C.

PRE-SHANG JADES
These ancient jades were probably
used in Neolithic rituals concerned
with death. The *cong* may have
represented the earthly powers.

The beginning of China

THE FIRSTS CHINESE DYNASTY to leave a historical record was the
Shang. The Shang kings ruled the greater part of northern China
from about 1650 to 1027 B.C. The Shang ruler was a kind of priest-
king, known as the Son of Heaven. He was believed to be vested
with all earthly powers and was expected to maintain good relations
between earth and the heavenly realm. The spirits of the royal
ancestors were consulted on every important decision. The king
alone possessed the authority to ask for their blessings, and he held
the power to ward off ancestral ill-will. Although the Shang rulers
had many slaves, they relied upon the labour of their mainly rural
population. The peasant farmers cultivated the land, took part in
royal hunts, and served as foot soldiers in the army.

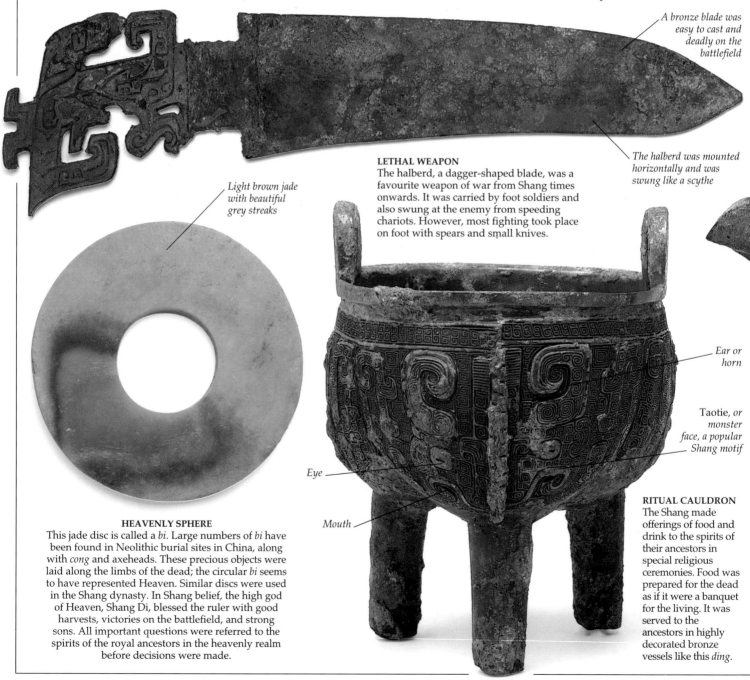

*A bronze blade was
easy to cast and
deadly on the
battlefield*

*The halberd was mounted
horizontally and was
swung like a scythe*

LETHAL WEAPON
The halberd, a dagger-shaped blade, was a
favourite weapon of war from Shang times
onwards. It was carried by foot soldiers and
also swung at the enemy from speeding
chariots. However, most fighting took place
on foot with spears and small knives.

*Light brown jade
with beautiful
grey streaks*

*Ear or
horn*

Taotie, or
monster
face, a popular
Shang motif

Eye

Mouth

HEAVENLY SPHERE
This jade disc is called a *bi*. Large numbers of *bi* have
been found in Neolithic burial sites in China, along
with *cong* and axeheads. These precious objects were
laid along the limbs of the dead; the circular *bi* seems
to have represented Heaven. Similar discs were used
in the Shang dynasty. In Shang belief, the high god
of Heaven, Shang Di, blessed the ruler with good
harvests, victories on the battlefield, and strong
sons. All important questions were referred to the
spirits of the royal ancestors in the heavenly realm
before decisions were made.

RITUAL CAULDRON
The Shang made
offerings of food and
drink to the spirits of
their ancestors in
special religious
ceremonies. Food was
prepared for the dead
as if it were a banquet
for the living. It was
served to the
ancestors in highly
decorated bronze
vessels like this *ding*.

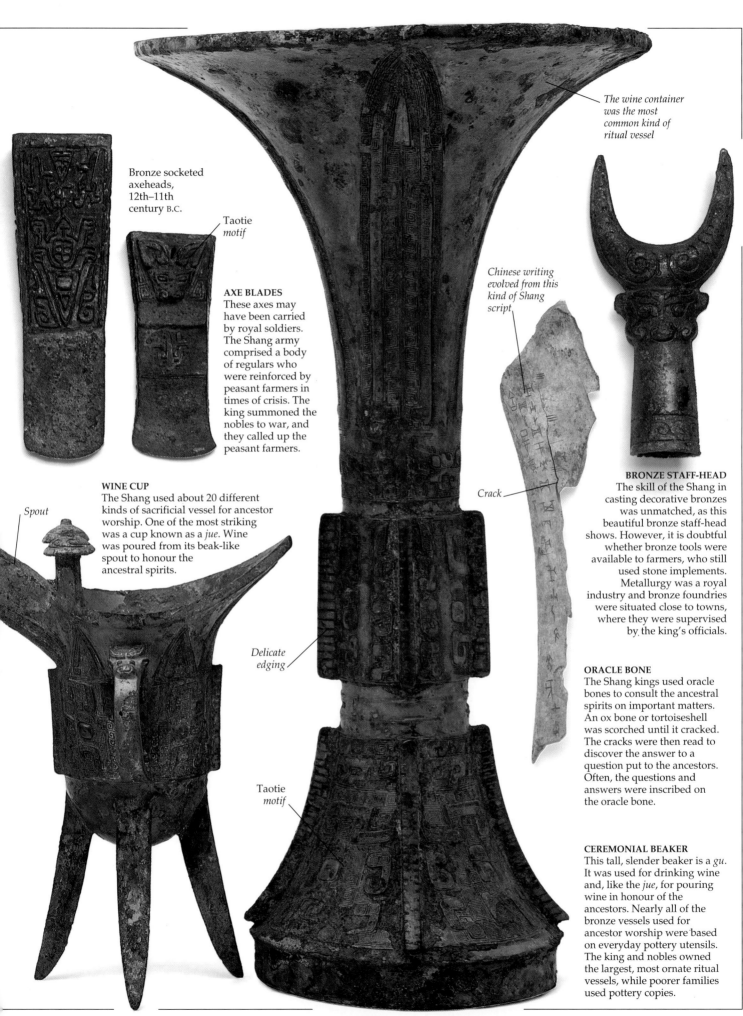

The wine container was the most common kind of ritual vessel

Bronze socketed axeheads, 12th–11th century B.C.

Taotie motif

AXE BLADES
These axes may have been carried by royal soldiers. The Shang army comprised a body of regulars who were reinforced by peasant farmers in times of crisis. The king summoned the nobles to war, and they called up the peasant farmers.

WINE CUP
The Shang used about 20 different kinds of sacrificial vessel for ancestor worship. One of the most striking was a cup known as a *jue*. Wine was poured from its beak-like spout to honour the ancestral spirits.

Spout

Delicate edging

Taotie motif

Chinese writing evolved from this kind of Shang script

Crack

BRONZE STAFF-HEAD
The skill of the Shang in casting decorative bronzes was unmatched, as this beautiful bronze staff-head shows. However, it is doubtful whether bronze tools were available to farmers, who still used stone implements. Metallurgy was a royal industry and bronze foundries were situated close to towns, where they were supervised by the king's officials.

ORACLE BONE
The Shang kings used oracle bones to consult the ancestral spirits on important matters. An ox bone or tortoiseshell was scorched until it cracked. The cracks were then read to discover the answer to a question put to the ancestors. Often, the questions and answers were inscribed on the oracle bone.

CEREMONIAL BEAKER
This tall, slender beaker is a *gu*. It was used for drinking wine and, like the *jue*, for pouring wine in honour of the ancestors. Nearly all of the bronze vessels used for ancestor worship were based on everyday pottery utensils. The king and nobles owned the largest, most ornate ritual vessels, while poorer families used pottery copies.

The teachings of Confucius

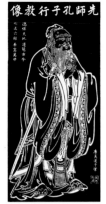

Confucius, the "uncrowned emperor" of China; his ideas shaped Chinese thought for several millennia

CONFUCIUS BELIEVED that the early years of the Zhou dynasty (1027–256 B.C.) were golden years of social harmony. In his own lifetime (551–479 B.C.) Confucius saw only growing disorder. The king's authority was greatly reduced as ambitious lords fought each other for power. This increasing turmoil led Confucius to develop a new moral outlook. It was based on kindness, respect, and the strength of the family. He said that a good ruler should set an example by dealing fairly with his subjects, using force only as a last resort. In return, subjects had a duty to respect and obey their ruler. Confucius believed that family relationships should be governed by the same principles of mutual respect, since strong families formed the basis of a stable society. He summed up his philosophy when he said: "Let the prince be a prince, the minister a minister, the father a father, and the son a son." Confucius encouraged ancestor worship because it strengthened family loyalties. As a result, the Chinese came to see themselves as part of a great family that encompassed not only the living, but also the dead and the unborn.

Large bronze bell, 6th–5th century B.C.

Bell was hung on a loop to allow it to vibrate clearly

ZHOU CHIMES
The Chinese believed the music of bells calmed the mind and aided thought. On hearing a piece of ritual music, Confucius was inspired to spurn worldly comforts and live on water and rice for three months.

Bell had no clapper inside; it was struck on the outside like a gong

Ear

Spiky horn

Horse-like face

RITES OF PASSAGE
Confucius had good reason to regard the first Zhou kings as ideal rulers. After the death of the last Shang king in 1027 B.C., the victorious Zhou leader, Wu, showed proper respect for the fallen royal house by arranging for the continuation of ancestral rites. This sacrificial vessel was used for ancestor worship in the early Zhou period.

Side view

Zhou bronze ritual vessel, or *gui*, 11th-century B.C.

Handle in the form of a mythical beast

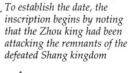

To establish the date, the inscription begins by noting that the Zhou king had been attacking the remnants of the defeated Shang kingdom

The script used to inscribe ritual vessels evolved into one of the most renowned forms of early Chinese writing

Overhead view

A MESSAGE TO THE ANCESTORS
An inscription inside this sacrificial vessel records the grant of territory or office to a friend of the Duke of Kang, a brother of the Zhou king Wu. Placing inscriptions inside ritual vessels was common practice among Zhou nobles. They recorded honours and gifts bestowed upon them by the king. The Zhou nobles believed that their ancestors would learn of their achievements when the vessels were used in the rituals of ancestor worship.

A DISTINGUISHED ANCESTOR
Ancestor worship became an important Chinese tradition. Offerings were made to the ancestors at the festival of Qingming once a year. This clay epitaph tablet stood in front of the tomb of Wang Yuanzhi, a senior administrator in the civil service who died in A.D. 571. The tablet served as a reminder to Wang Yuanzhi's descendants of his distinguished career. They would have made offerings before it during Qingming.

FEARSOME GUARDIAN
Relatives conducted the annual rite of ancestor worship at the entrance to their ancestor's tomb. From the Han dynasty onwards, every wealthy person had a brick-built underground tomb decorated with pressed bricks or wall paintings. The tomb was covered by a mound and enclosed within a sacred area. Ancestor worshippers approached along a spirit path lined with carvings of animals and sometimes people.

Tomb guardian, or qitou, Tang dynasty

Characters incised in clay, then painted red

FABULOUS TOMB ANIMAL
Confucius was against slavery and human or animal sacrifices. Under his influence, it became common practice to place pottery figures inside tombs instead of living slaves and animals. This strange pottery animal was found in a tomb that dates from the 4th century A.D. It was probably intended to ward off evil influences.

Painted mane

Snaky tail

Cow-like body

Cloven hoof

13

The art of war

THREE CENTURIES OF BRUTAL WARFARE marked the decline of the Zhou dynasty. The Zhou became unable to control disputes among the great lords, and by 481 B.C. China had separated into seven warring states. Battles became large-scale contests with armoured infantry, crossbowmen, cavalry, and chariots. Thousands of men were killed or wounded. At the battle of Chang Ping in 260 B.C., over half a million men are known to have fallen. During this period Sun Zi wrote *The Art of War*, the world's oldest military handbook, which gave advice to nobles on the practice of warfare. Eventually the north-western state of Qin was victorious and, in 221 B.C., united the feuding lords under a single empire. In later years, the military declined in status. The civil service grew in importance and the gentler ideas of Confucianism prevailed.

Guan Di the Confucian god of war, worshipped for his ability to prevent conflicts as well as for his heroic character

Harness ornament fitted along the horse's cheek

Taotie, *or monster face, decoration*

Scabbard and dagger, 7th–6th century B.C.

Gold harness ornaments with *taotie* design, 7th–6th century B.C.

HARNESS ORNAMENTS
These ornate harness attachments decorated the the harnesses of cavalry horses. Although battles largely became contests between massed ranks of foot soldiers, or infantry, the cavalry were still used for lightning attacks and for the defence of the infantry's flanks.

SWORD PLAY
Military success was displayed in fine weapons, such as this bronze dagger and sword. However, bronze weapons never achieved the same status that the medieval sword did in Europe. In imperial China, peaceful Confucian virtues were revered over the art of warfare.

SHOW OF STRENGTH
This horse frontlet fitted along the nose of a chariot horse. Both harnesses and chariots were decorated to heighten the magnificent spectacle of the chariots in battle. These splendid vehicles were important status symbols. They were buried with their owners, along with the horses and charioteers.

Bronze horse bit, Han dynasty

Bronze nose-guard for a chariot horse

Bronze axle cap protected the axle of a chariot wheel

HORSEPOWER
This delicate bit was probably worn by a cavalry horse in the Han dynasty. Chinese cavalrymen rode the small Mongolian pony until the Han emperor Wu Di obtained bigger horses from Central Asia in 101 B.C. This greatly improved the strength of the cavalry. The larger horses were faster and could carry more heavily armoured men.

ANCIENT AXLE CAPS
Chariots were made of wood and were pulled by two or four horses. Their wheels raised them high above the ground. They usually carried three men: a charioteer, an archer, and a halberdier. The management of a chariot was considered an essential skill for a noble.

Sword, 4th century B.C.

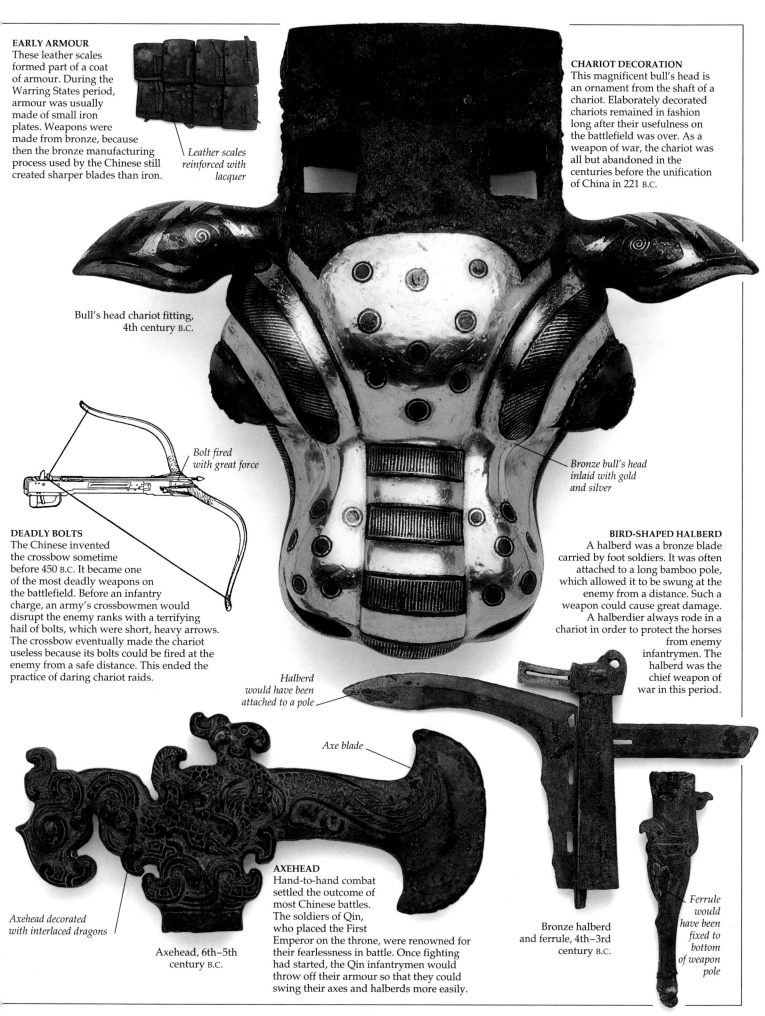

EARLY ARMOUR
These leather scales formed part of a coat of armour. During the Warring States period, armour was usually made of small iron plates. Weapons were made from bronze, because then the bronze manufacturing process used by the Chinese still created sharper blades than iron.

Leather scales reinforced with lacquer

Bull's head chariot fitting, 4th century B.C.

CHARIOT DECORATION
This magnificent bull's head is an ornament from the shaft of a chariot. Elaborately decorated chariots remained in fashion long after their usefulness on the battlefield was over. As a weapon of war, the chariot was all but abandoned in the centuries before the unification of China in 221 B.C.

Bolt fired with great force

Bronze bull's head inlaid with gold and silver

DEADLY BOLTS
The Chinese invented the crossbow sometime before 450 B.C. It became one of the most deadly weapons on the battlefield. Before an infantry charge, an army's crossbowmen would disrupt the enemy ranks with a terrifying hail of bolts, which were short, heavy arrows. The crossbow eventually made the chariot useless because its bolts could be fired at the enemy from a safe distance. This ended the practice of daring chariot raids.

Halberd would have been attached to a pole

Axe blade

BIRD-SHAPED HALBERD
A halberd was a bronze blade carried by foot soldiers. It was often attached to a long bamboo pole, which allowed it to be swung at the enemy from a distance. Such a weapon could cause great damage. A halberdier always rode in a chariot in order to protect the horses from enemy infantrymen. The halberd was the chief weapon of war in this period.

Axehead decorated with interlaced dragons

Axehead, 6th–5th century B.C.

AXEHEAD
Hand-to-hand combat settled the outcome of most Chinese battles. The soldiers of Qin, who placed the First Emperor on the throne, were renowned for their fearlessness in battle. Once fighting had started, the Qin infantrymen would throw off their armour so that they could swing their axes and halberds more easily.

Bronze halberd and ferrule, 4th–3rd century B.C.

Ferrule would have been fixed to bottom of weapon pole

The first emperor of China

Jade dragon ornaments; the dragon was the adopted symbol of the First Emperor

IN 221 B.C. THE CHINESE EMPIRE was formed. The Qin soldiers defeated the last of their enemies and united the "warring states" under one leader, Zheng. To show his supremacy over the kings he had vanquished, Zheng took the title of First Sovereign Qin Emperor, or Qin Shi Huangdi. The empire took its name from the Qin (pronounced "Chin") to become China. The First Emperor (221–207 B.C.) seems to have thought he would become immortal. He built an impressive tomb guarded by thousands of life-sized terracotta warriors, probably in the belief that he would remain a powerful man in the afterlife. His brief reign on earth was harsh. He used his subjects as slave labour to build the Great Wall and ruthlessly suppressed anyone who disagreed with him. But after the First Emperor's rule, the Chinese felt that unity was normal.

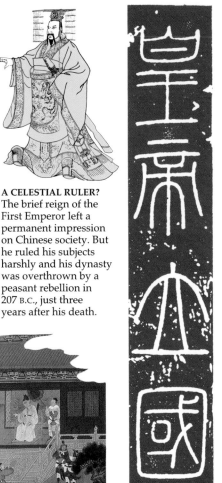

A CELESTIAL RULER?
The brief reign of the First Emperor left a permanent impression on Chinese society. But he ruled his subjects harshly and his dynasty was overthrown by a peasant rebellion in 207 B.C., just three years after his death.

THE TERRACOTTA ARMY
The ghostly army of terracotta soldiers, left, that guards the First Emperor's tomb is accompanied by life-size horses and chariots. No two soldiers have the same face – each is an individual portrait of a soldier from the Qin army. The soldiers once carried real weapons, but these were stolen by grave robbers after the fall of the Qin.

Clouds

Dragon roundel, probably used on a 19th-century imperial robe

Waves

WHAT'S IN A NAME?
This is the beginning of an inscription celebrating the unification of China by the First Emperor in 221 B.C. The top character is part of the First Emperor's title. It conveys the idea of divinity, or divine favour.

THE BURNING OF THE BOOKS
When scholars disagreed with his harsh acts, the First Emperor burned their books and executed those who spoke against him, as seen above. He was particularly displeased with followers of Confucius who pointed out how his policies differed from the ways of old. In 213 B.C., his chief minister announced: "No one is to use the past to discredit the present." Only books on agriculture, medicine, and oracles were spared the flames.

THE DRAGON KING
The association of Chinese emperors with the dragon was undoubtedly due to the First Emperor. The dragon became the First Emperor's emblem because it was divine lord of water, the lucky element of his people, the Qin.

GREAT BUILDING WORKS
The First Emperor used the forced labour of his subjects to carry out his extensive public works. These included the Great Wall, roads, and canals. The hardship suffered by the thousands of men who toiled on the Great Wall is still recalled in Chinese folksongs. To fund his projects, the First Emperor taxed his subjects heavily, which led to widespread suffering and starvation.

THE GREAT WALL OF CHINA
The First Emperor's greatest achievement was the construction of the Great Wall in about 214 B.C. It joined together a number of defensive walls aimed at keeping out the Xiongnu nomads. It is the longest structure ever built.

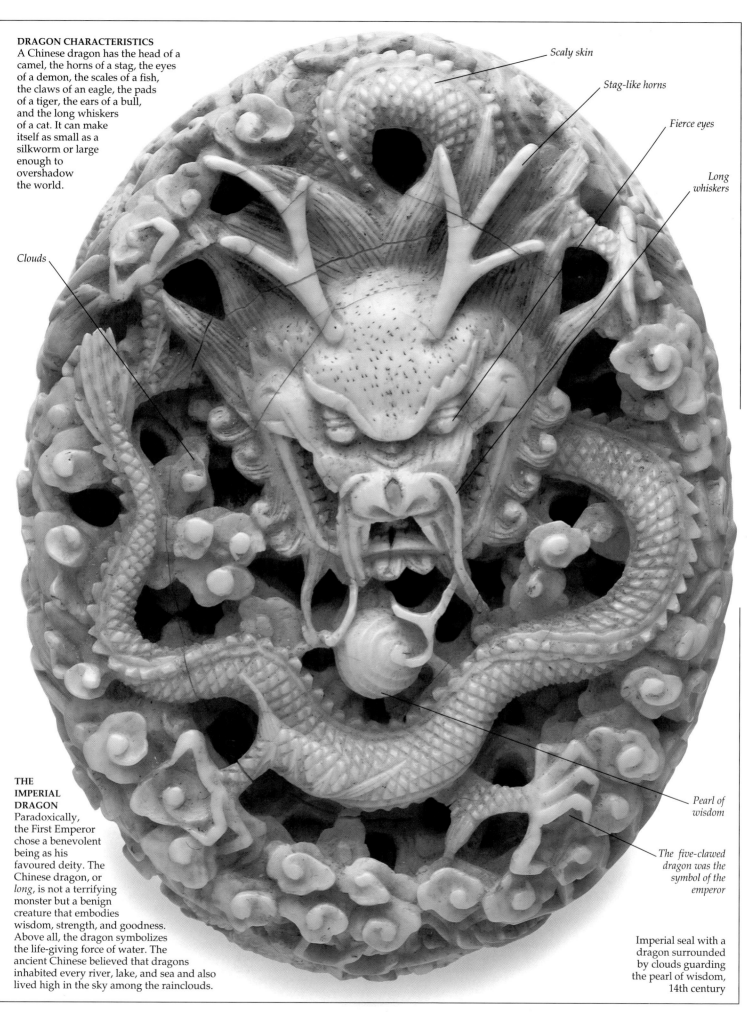

DRAGON CHARACTERISTICS
A Chinese dragon has the head of a camel, the horns of a stag, the eyes of a demon, the scales of a fish, the claws of an eagle, the pads of a tiger, the ears of a bull, and the long whiskers of a cat. It can make itself as small as a silkworm or large enough to overshadow the world.

Scaly skin

Stag-like horns

Fierce eyes

Long whiskers

Clouds

Pearl of wisdom

THE IMPERIAL DRAGON
Paradoxically, the First Emperor chose a benevolent being as his favoured deity. The Chinese dragon, or *long*, is not a terrifying monster but a benign creature that embodies wisdom, strength, and goodness. Above all, the dragon symbolizes the life-giving force of water. The ancient Chinese believed that dragons inhabited every river, lake, and sea and also lived high in the sky among the rainclouds.

The five-clawed dragon was the symbol of the emperor

Imperial seal with a dragon surrounded by clouds guarding the pearl of wisdom, 14th century

In the empire's service

THE EARLIEST MEMBERS of the imperial civil service were recruited by Gaozu (206–195 B.C.), the first Han emperor. Gaozu led one of the peasant armies that overthrew the Qin dynasty in 207 B.C. Although Gaozu was uneducated, when he came to power he realized the empire needed educated administrators. He gathered together scholars to form an imperial civil service, which was destined to run China for 2,000 years. In 124 B.C. the Han emperor Wu Di (140–87 B.C.) introduced examinations for civil servants and founded an imperial university where candidates studied the ancient Confucian classics. In later dynasties, a series of examinations took successful candidates from their local districts, through the provinces, to the imperial palace. Those who passed the top palace examinations could expect to be appointed as ministers or even marry princesses.

THE MOMENT OF TRUTH
These local magistrates are taking part in a civil service examination. At each level, only a few candidates passed. They answered questions on the Confucian classics, whose 431, 286 words had to be learned by heart. Reform of the curriculum was strongly opposed and it hardly changed through the centuries.

Long beard associated with old age and wisdom

19TH-CENTURY EXAM PAPER
This test paper shows a candidate's answer and his tutor's comments. Those who studied for an official career knew it involved long years of preparation, but the rewards were great. On receiving his results, an 8th-century graduate called Meng Jiao remarked: "The drudgery of yesterday is forgotten. Today the prospects are vast, and my heart is filled with joy!"

A WISE OFFICIAL
Qiu Jun, above, was a Ming official who persuaded the emperor to strengthen the Great Wall against the Manchus. His advice was well-founded. The Manchus invaded China in 1644.

18th-century figure in official garb

Circles indicate praise for calligraphy

THE PASSING OUT PARADE
The special slate or document held by this official would have been carried on formal occasions, such as the splendid graduation ceremony of successful examination candidates. In the imperial palace, top graduates received their degrees and bowed to the emperor.

A NEW CURRICULUM
The Song minister Wang Anshi, above, altered the civil service examinations so that a mastery of technical subjects would be favoured over learning by heart. This reform lasted only briefly.

Plaque was sewn on to official robes

OFFICIAL PLAQUE
This beautiful gold plaque is decorated with imperial five-clawed dragons and semi-precious stones. Such an expensive badge of rank may have been worn by an imperial minister or a prince during the Ming dynasty.

THE DANGERS OF CHEATING
This handkerchief covered with model exam answers would have made a clever crib. However, cheating in the imperial examinations was not only difficult, but dangerous. Candidates sat the provincial examinations in open-doored cells inside walled compounds. Soldiers in watchtowers made sure that no cribs were smuggled in. When the emperor Xian Feng learned of cheating in the palace examinations of 1859, he beheaded the examiners responsible for the cheating, banished the administrators, and took away the qualifications of the guilty graduates.

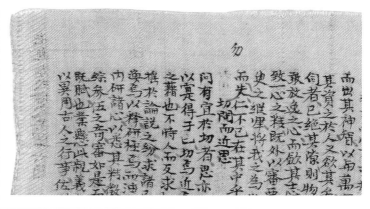

Continued on next page

A civil service career

Graduate civil servants had secured jobs in the most honourable and best rewarded career in China. They took posts in local, provincial, or national government. Competition to join the civil service became so intense during the final centuries of the empire that the odds against succeeding in the top, palace examinations were as high as 3,000 to one.

A PREFECT IN HIS COURT
The bulk of the work in the civil service was carried out in the local districts, or prefectures, by prefects. A prefect, or *ling*, had to enforce law and order, register individuals and property, collect taxes, store grain against times of famine, organize labour for public works, supervise schools, and judge civil and criminal cases. The area for which a prefect was responsible consisted of a walled city or town and its surrounding villages and farmland.

Celestial clouds

Senior official

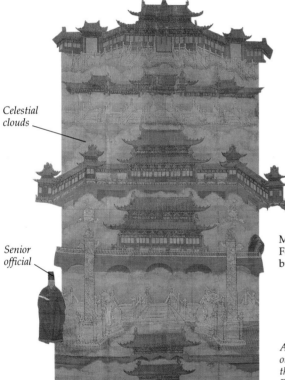

Ming painting on silk of the Forbidden City, which was built in the early 15th century

An official greets others outside the gates of the Forbidden City

COURT NECKLACE
The clothes and jewellery worn by officials were an indication of rank and therefore followed strict guidelines. This kind of necklace was worn only by officials in the top five ranks during the Qing dynasty. The design was based on the Buddhist rosary.

Subsidiary string of 10 beads

Large beads called Buddha heads divide the smaller beads into groups of 27

Ivory court necklace, early 20th century

Cap made from black velvet

Bronze finial

GATEWAY FOR THE CHOSEN FEW
This painting shows the Forbidden City, the splendid palace built in Beijing by the Ming emperor Yong Le. Only senior officials and ministers could enter its Meridian Gate, seen here with its triple archways. The most senior official in the empire was called the Grand Tutor in deference to Confucius.

BADGE OF RANK
The rank of this military official from the Qing dynasty is indicated by the embroidered badge on the front of his surcoat, or *pufu*. His tiger insignia shows that he was a fourth-rank official.

OFFICIAL HEADWARE
Once the Qing dynasty was firmly established, the black hat with side flaps worn by Ming civil servants was replaced by the Manchu cap. This cap had a finial to indicate rank; it could be made from bronze, glass, crystal, coral, or jade.

MASSED RANKS

The size of the civil service under the different dynasties is not always clear. However, in the Han dynasty the civil service was known to contain 135,285 officials. By the Ming dynasty this number had grown to 180,000. When officials were crowded together, it was often difficult to see which ranks they belonged to. Therefore, from the Ming dynasty onwards, the rank of a civil servant was indicated by a large badge sewn on to his surcoat. Each of the nine civil service ranks was identified by a different bird. These two badges are from the Qing dynasty. The white crane, above, was the official insignia of the first rank, and the egret, right, signified the sixth.

SEAL OF APPROVAL

Every document in China was stamped with a seal. This 18th-century bronze seal belonged to the civil service department responsible for supplying water to the capital, Beijing. It is inscribed with both Manchu and Chinese scripts, a reminder of the foreign origin of the last imperial house, the Manchu, or Qing dynasty.

A land of invention

Pocket compass

SOME OF THE WORLD'S GREATEST INVENTIONS came from China. Throughout its imperial history, emperors encouraged the development of science and technology, and for centuries China led other nations in these areas. In the Middle Ages many Chinese inventions were carried along the Silk Road to Europe, where some had an enormous impact. In time, paper and printing dramatically improved communications; gunpowder changed the way in which battles were fought; a harness for draft animals revolutionized agriculture; and boats equipped with the magnetic compass, the stern-post rudder, and water-tight buoyancy chambers were able to embark on great voyages of discovery. Other Chinese inventions that made the world a different place were paper money, clockwork, silk, porcelain, fireworks, kites, umbrellas, and the wheelbarrow.

A WATER-POWERED BLAST FURNACE
China was the first country in the world to develop iron casting in the 6th century B.C. This skill was refined in the 1st century A.D. by an unknown official who invented a water-powered metallurgical blowing machine. The machine, pictured on the right, produced a steady blast of heat that greatly improved cast iron production. It helped increase the output of the state-owned iron industry and may have led to the first production of steel.

THE "EARTHQUAKE WEATHERCOCK"
The first instrument for monitoring earthquakes was invented in A.D. 130 by Zhang Heng, director of astrology in the late Han court. Zhang Heng's invention, below, could detect an earthquake and indicate its direction from the capital, Luoyang. The original apparatus was a huge bronze machine that measured 2 metres (6 feet) across. An earthquake tremor caused a mechanism inside the machine to release a ball from the side of the machine farthest away from the earthquake's epicentre. This notified the emperor of the direction of the disaster.

FINDING THE RIGHT DIRECTION
The magnetic compass was an ancient Chinese invention. Compasses were first used in town planning to make sure that new houses faced in a direction that was deemed to be in harmony with nature. Later the compass was used for navigation at sea. These 19th-century compasses are from the port of Canton.

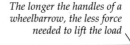

The longer the handles of a wheelbarrow, the less force needed to lift the load

Bronze ball released from dragon's mouth

Toad catches the ball

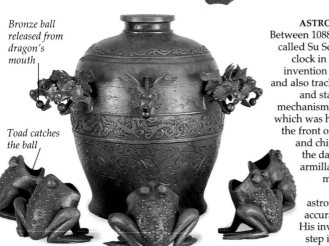

ASTRONOMICAL CLOCKWORK
Between 1088 and 1092, a civil servant called Su Song built an astronomical clock in Kaifeng. This marvellous invention could tell the time of day and also track the orbits of the planets and stars. It ran on a clockwork mechanism driven by a waterwheel, which was housed inside a tower. At the front of the tower, small figures and chimes marked the hours of the day. On top, a huge bronze armillary sphere monitored the movements of the planets. Readings from Su Song's astronomical clock enabled an accurate calendar to be drawn. His invention was an important step in the development of the mechanical clock.

Armillary sphere

Puppet holds up a plaque telling the time

STEERING A STRAIGHT COURSE

The stern-post rudder was invented between 205 B.C.and A.D. 220. It made the steering of large vessels possible for the first time. Chinese junks of 1,500 tonnes could carry huge loads long before such large ships were built in Europe.

Shield to protect soldier

Multiple gun releases a hail of bullets

Ming soldier firing a multiple gun

GUNPOWDER

Chinese alchemists discovered gunpowder in the 8th century while they were carrying out experiments to find the elixir of life. By the 10th century, gunpowder was being used to make fireworks and weapons. The Chinese invented the gun, the rocket, the bomb, and the mine. The Song army used guns against the invading Mongols in the early 13th century, but they were eventually overpowered by the greater might of the Mongol army.

Ocean-going junk

Rudder

One-dollar note, 1906

Basket for carrying loads

THE PAPER REVOLUTION

Paper-making was perfected in China in A.D. 105 by an imperial official called Cai Lun. The first paper was made from pulped silk waste. Later hemp, bark, or bamboo were used. Paper was a necessary forerunner of widescale printing, and it played an important part in the spread of books and the growth of literacy in China. Paper money first appeared in the 11th century.

The wheelbarrow was sometimes fitted with a sail to harness wind power

THE WHEELBARROW

The Chinese invented the wheelbarrow between 221 B.C. and A.D. 265. This large handcart enabled a single person to transport a heavy load, which led to its Chinese name of the "wooden ox".

A sturdy wheel lifts the load above the ground

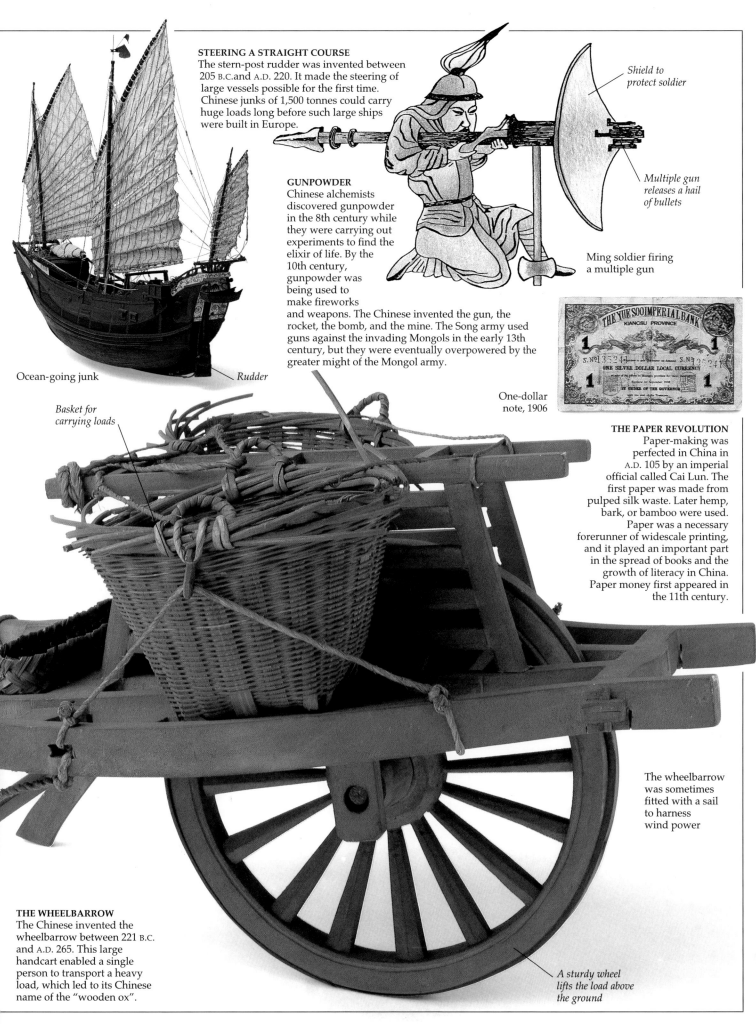

Paper, printing, and books

PAPER AND PRINTING were possibly the most important Chinese inventions. Credit for the successful manufacture of paper is given to Cai Lun, head of the imperial workshops in A.D. 105. The first paper was made from silk rags, but later other fibrous materials were used, such as bamboo, hemp, and mulberry bark. There was a great demand for paper from the Han civil service and it was soon mass-produced in government factories. Large-scale woodblock printing was developed in the 9th century, which increased the availability of reading material. By the end of the Tang dynasty, bookshops were trading in every Chinese city. Movable type was invented by a printer called Bi Sheng in the Song dynasty, but because at least 80,000 separate type symbols were needed, it did not entirely replace block printing.

Bamboo symbolized strength and flexibility

BAMBOO BOOKS
The first Chinese books were made from strips of bamboo, such as the ones pictured right, which were tied together in a bundle. These early books were unwieldy to use and took up a lot of storage space.

PAPER-MAKING
Before the paper-making process could begin, the raw material was softened by being soaked in water. After that, it was boiled and pounded to form a pulp. To make a sheet of paper, a fine screen was dipped into the pulp to gather a thin film of fibres. The screen was pressed to remove the water, then left to dry on a heated wall. When dry, the finished sheet of paper was peeled off the screen.

SEAL PRINTS
Seals, which date back to the Zhou dynasty, were the first form of printing used in China. They were impressed on official documents, personal correspondence, and works of art. Seals were carved or moulded from stone, wood, horn, bronze, or ceramics. This 15th-century soapstone seal was engraved by a famous Ming calligrapher.

Soaking the bamboo

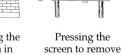

Dipping the screen in the vat

Pressing the screen to remove the water

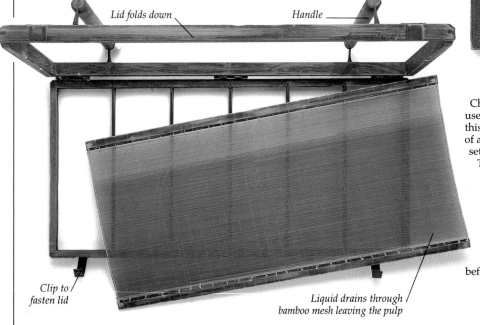

Lid folds down

Handle

Clip to fasten lid

Liquid drains through bamboo mesh leaving the pulp

PAPER MOULD
Chinese paper-makers used paper moulds like this one, which consists of a fine bamboo screen set in a wooden frame. The mould is dipped into a vat of mushy pulp and shaken gently to settle the fibres on the screen. The screen is then taken out and pressed to remove the excess water before being left to dry.

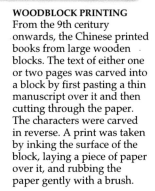

WOODBLOCK PRINTING
From the 9th century onwards, the Chinese printed books from large wooden blocks. The text of either one or two pages was carved into a block by first pasting a thin manuscript over it and then cutting through the paper. The characters were carved in reverse. A print was taken by inking the surface of the block, laying a piece of paper over it, and rubbing the paper gently with a brush.

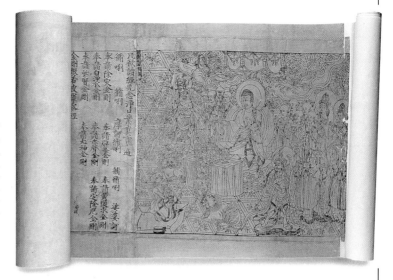

ON A SCROLL
The first Chinese books made from paper were rolled into long scrolls. They were usually hand-written by scholars. As in modern China, the text was written in vertical columns and read from right to left.

PRAYERS IN PRINT
This Buddhist text, called the *Diamond Sutra*, is the earliest known printed book. It was made in China in A.D. 868 using woodblock printing. Buddhists produced thousands of copies of sacred texts and prayers. The *Diamond Sutra* was made for free distribution.

Book cover decorated with colourful chrysanthemums

STYLISH NOTEPAPER
This collection of decorated letter papers is a fine example of coloured woodblock printing, which flourished in 16th-century China. It was produced by the Ten Bamboo Studio in 1644. Scholars used beautifully designed letter papers for decorative letters. The delicate illustrations were intended to be written over.

20th-century facsimile of a compendium of letter papers from the Ten Bamboo Studio

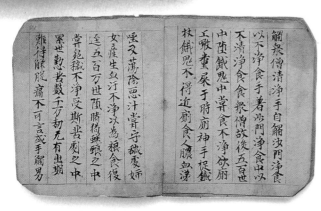

EMERGENCY MANUAL
Large-scale printing in the 10th century made books readily available in China for the first time. The proliferation of books greatly increased the spread of literacy. The most popular printed material was Buddhist texts and prayers. This 1,000-year-old booklet contains a Buddhist prayer called the *Lotus Sutra*. It is a prayer for use in emergencies that calls on the help of friendly spirits.

Illustration from a letter paper

The Three Ways

In IMPERIAL CHINA, RELIGIOUS BELIEFS were divided into the "three ways" of Confucianism, Daoism, and Buddhism. Throughout its long history, China was tolerant of all religions. Although there were disagreements over religious principles, few people were persecuted for their beliefs. In this respect, the Chinese empire was unique among civilizations. Confucianism and Daoism emerged in the Warring States period. Against the backdrop of constant warfare, these two religions encouraged more peaceful ways of being. Buddhism came to China from India in the 1st century A.D., and its gentle teachings became popular in the troubled centuries that followed the end of the Han dynasty. The return of strong government under the Tang emperors (618–906) led to the decline of Buddhism and the revival of Confucianism. Nevertheless, Buddhism had become firmly rooted in Chinese culture and became China's most popular belief.

Lao Zi is always depicted as an old man

LAO ZI
Daoists were followers of Lao Zi, or the "Old Philosopher" (born c. 604 B.C.), who believed that people should live in harmony with nature. He explained his ideas in a book called the *Daodejing*. Lao Zi wanted people to lead simple lives that did not disrupt the balance of the natural world. He disliked the importance Confucius placed on duty to family and state because he did not believe in man-made rules and regulations. Daoism was represented by the yin yang sign, which reflects natural harmony.

Zhongli Quan, chief of the eight immortals, who could raise the dead with a wave of his fan

Tortoise, a symbol of luck and wisdom

Flute

Sacred scroll

Fan

THE GENTLE PROTECTOR
Kuanyin was the Buddhist goddess of mercy. Her name means "She Who Hears Prayers", and she is often portrayed as the protector of children. Kuanyin was a Chinese transformation of the Indian male god Avalokitesvara. This is just one of the many changes the Chinese made to Indian Buddhism. In China, Kuanyin was the greatest Buddhist deity.

THE HEIGHT OF BEAUTY
A pagoda is a sacred Buddhist tower. Pagodas have from three to 15 tiers and are usually exquisitely decorated. The Chinese believed that a pagoda brought good fortune to the area surrounding it.

Zhang Guolao an immortal who could make himself invisible

THE MYSTERIES OF THE IMMORTALS
Daoists thought that it was possible to discover the elixir of life and become immortal. They worshipped eight figures whom they believed had achieved immortality. These mysterious immortals, or *xian*, lived in remote mountains. They were said to have supernatural powers, such as the power to turn objects into gold, become invisible, make flowers bloom instantly, or raise the dead.

Han Xiangzi, patron of musicians, who could make flowers blossom instantly

Ivory figures, Ming dynasty, 16th–17th century

A GUARDIAN FROM THE SPIRIT WORLD
A Bodhisattva, or "Enlightened Being", is a kind of Buddhist god. Bodhisattvas were said to have postponed their own hope of eternal peace, or nirvana, in order to help other people. Kuanyin, the goddess of mercy, was the greatest Chinese Bodhisattva, but there were many others that Buddhists could call upon when they needed help.

Stucco head of a Bodhisattva, 8th–9th century A.D.

Crown

CONFUCIUS
The great Chinese thinker Confucius (551–479 B.C.) taught people to show respect for one another. He said that a good ruler should cherish his subjects and they should honour him. He also believed that respect within the family was very important because a stable society was based on strong families. The Daoists did not agree with Confucius. In his own defence Confucius said: "They dislike me because I want to reform society, but if we are not to live with our fellow men with whom can we live? We cannot live with animals. If society was as it ought to be, I should not seek to change it."

Modern Buddhist image for domestic use

Auriole shows the emanation of holiness from the Buddha

Buddha seated on a sacred lotus

BUDDHA
Buddhists follow the teachings of Buddha (born c. 563 B.C.), a north Indian prince who devoted his life to a search for personal peace, or enlightenment. His name means "Enlightened One". Buddha believed that by giving up worldly desires, such as good food and fine clothes, a blissful state called nirvana could be achieved. In nirvana there was freedom from the sorrows of the world. Indian belief at that time held that people were reborn many times. If a person had lived badly in former lives, they might be reborn in animal or insect form. Buddha said that by reaching nirvana, this endless cycle of rebirth could be broken.

Head blends male and female characteristics

Health and medicine

TRADITIONAL CHINESE MEDICINE is based on the use of herbs, acupuncture, and a balanced diet. It combines ancient philosophy with practical skills. According to Chinese belief, a person falls ill when the two opposing forces of yin and yang become unbalanced in the body. Doctors use acupuncture and herbal remedies to re-channel these natural energies. Chinese interest in medicine dates back over 4,000 years. In ancient times, the Daoists believed that it was possible to find the elixir of life, which would make people immortal. Concern with health also came from the need to produce strong sons who would ensure the survival of the family. From the Tang dynasty onwards, Chinese doctors were regularly examined on their medical expertise. In 1111, the entire knowledge of the medical profession was compiled in a vast encyclopedia. This great work listed all the known diseases, with their symptoms, diagnoses, and treatments. It became the standard reference book for Chinese medicine.

Liquorice root, or *gan cao*

Chinese hawthorn, or *shan zha*

Smoked plums, or *wu mei*

VITAL NOURISHMENT
The Chinese have always believed a balanced diet to be the basis of good health. The ingredients above make up a nourishing herbal drink said to improve the appetite and clear the chest.

Coin sword from the Qing dynasty, placed by the bed of a sick person to ward off bad spirits

10th-century acupuncture chart showing some of the main needle points in the arm

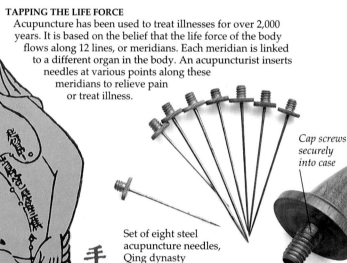

TAPPING THE LIFE FORCE
Acupuncture has been used to treat illnesses for over 2,000 years. It is based on the belief that the life force of the body flows along 12 lines, or meridians. Each meridian is linked to a different organ in the body. An acupuncturist inserts needles at various points along these meridians to relieve pain or treat illness.

Set of eight steel acupuncture needles, Qing dynasty

Cap screws securely into case

NATURAL PAIN RELIEF
This set of needles belonged to a 19th-century acupuncturist. In the 20th century, doctors have discovered that acupuncture can be used as an anaesthetic for surgery. When acupuncture is used during an operation, the patient remains conscious and feels little or no pain. Scientists believe acupuncture works by stimulating the release of endorphins, the brain's natural painkillers.

Mahogany case for storing needles

HEAT TREATMENT
Moxibustion is a pain-relief treatment that uses heat produced by burning dried mugwort, or *moxa*. Acupuncture and moxibustion are often used together. An acupuncture needle can be fitted with a small cap in which *moxa* is burned. The heat is carried into the body by the needle. Burning *moxa* sticks can also be used to apply heat to certain parts of the body.

Moxa stick

Moxa wool

Moxa *burned in cap*

Modern acupuncture needles with a cap for *moxa* wool

Lighted end of moxa *stick* is held over painful area

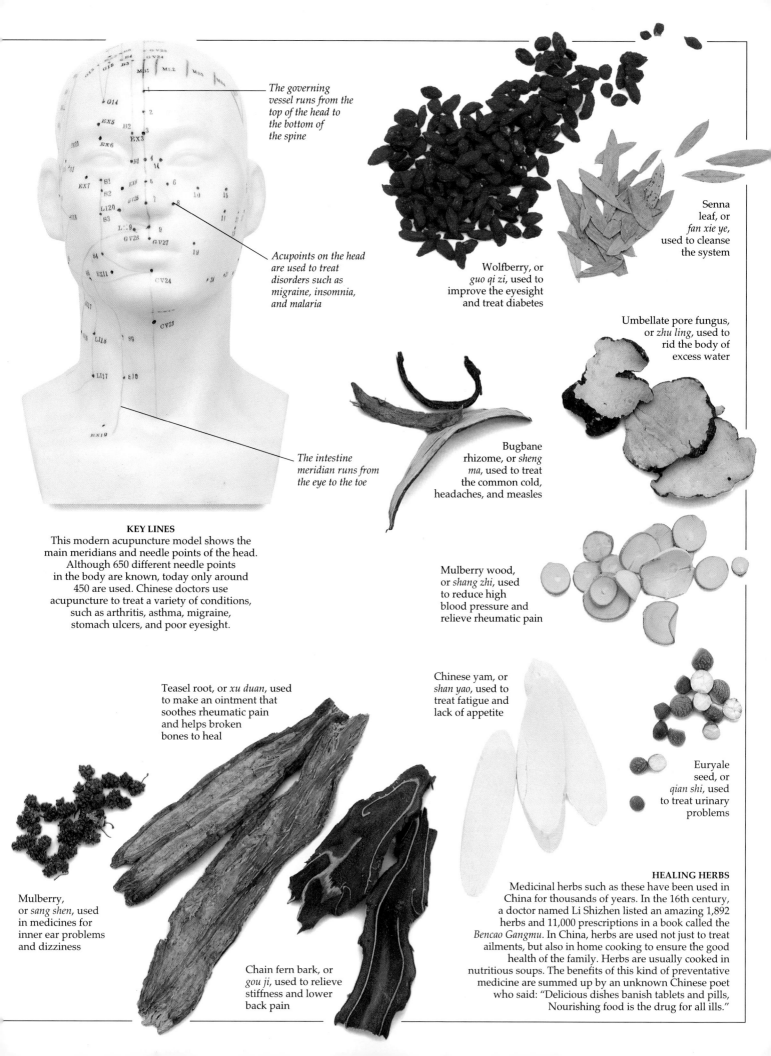

The governing vessel runs from the top of the head to the bottom of the spine

Acupoints on the head are used to treat disorders such as migraine, insomnia, and malaria

The intestine meridian runs from the eye to the toe

KEY LINES

This modern acupuncture model shows the main meridians and needle points of the head. Although 650 different needle points in the body are known, today only around 450 are used. Chinese doctors use acupuncture to treat a variety of conditions, such as arthritis, asthma, migraine, stomach ulcers, and poor eyesight.

Wolfberry, or *guo qi zi*, used to improve the eyesight and treat diabetes

Senna leaf, or *fan xie ye*, used to cleanse the system

Umbellate pore fungus, or *zhu ling*, used to rid the body of excess water

Bugbane rhizome, or *sheng ma*, used to treat the common cold, headaches, and measles

Mulberry wood, or *shang zhi*, used to reduce high blood pressure and relieve rheumatic pain

Chinese yam, or *shan yao*, used to treat fatigue and lack of appetite

Euryale seed, or *qian shi*, used to treat urinary problems

Teasel root, or *xu duan*, used to make an ointment that soothes rheumatic pain and helps broken bones to heal

Mulberry, or *sang shen*, used in medicines for inner ear problems and dizziness

Chain fern bark, or *gou ji*, used to relieve stiffness and lower back pain

HEALING HERBS

Medicinal herbs such as these have been used in China for thousands of years. In the 16th century, a doctor named Li Shizhen listed an amazing 1,892 herbs and 11,000 prescriptions in a book called the *Bencao Gangmu*. In China, herbs are used not just to treat ailments, but also in home cooking to ensure the good health of the family. Herbs are usually cooked in nutritious soups. The benefits of this kind of preventative medicine are summed up by an unknown Chinese poet who said: "Delicious dishes banish tablets and pills, Nourishing food is the drug for all ills."

The Three Perfections

CALLIGRAPHY, POETRY, AND PAINTING were known as the "three perfections". The combination of these arts was considered the height of artistic expression. They were usually combined in the form of a poetically inspired landscape painting with beautiful calligraphy running down one side. From the Song dynasty (960–1279) onwards, the practice of the three perfections was seen as the greatest accomplishment of an educated person. The Song emperor Hui Zong (1101–25) led the way towards transforming writing into an art form. He developed an elegant style of calligraphy called "slender gold". Hui Zong was also a gifted poet and painter, and the arts flourished under his reign.

IN THE BEGINNING
Legend has it that Chinese writing was invented over 4,000 years ago by Cang Jie, an official of the mythical Yellow Emperor. He devised written characters from the tracks of birds and animals. The legend says that "all the spirits cried out in agony, as the innermost secrets of nature were revealed".

Water well to dip ink stick into

Soft, springy brush tip probably made from wolf hair

THE DAILY GRIND
Calligraphers produced their own ink by grinding ink sticks or cakes into a small amount of water on an inkstone. Inkstones were made from stone or pottery. Smooth, hard stones were favoured because they allowed the ink to be finely ground to make smooth ink. This inkstone from the Qing dynasty is made from Duan stone and carved in the shape of two fungi.

Ink stick is rubbed on the smooth part of the inkstone

Ink cake decorated with a legendary animal

Classical garden depicted in mother-of-pearl inlay

Box lined with tortoiseshell

CARBON COPY
Ink was made by mixing pine soot with lampblack obtained from other burned plants. This mixture was combined with glue and moulded into a stick or cake. Ink sticks and cakes were often decorated with calligraphy or moulded into the shapes of dragons and birds copied from mythology.

19th-century ink box

COLOURED INKS
Both calligraphers and painters used inks. In the Song dynasty, coloured inks were made by adding materials such as pearl powder, ground jade, and camphor to ink. Later other pigments were used: indigo for blue, lead for white, cinnabar for red, and malachite for green.

Modern coloured ink sticks embossed with gold dragons

A TREASURED POSSESSION
This beautiful writing brush from the Ming dynasty is made from lacquered wood and inlaid with mother-of-pearl. It was usual for everyday writing implements to be highly decorated. In the 10th century the brushes, paper, ink, and inkstone used by a calligrapher became known as "the four treasures of the scholar's studio".

This character means "brilliant"; it comes from a poem composed around 1120

Each stroke must be drawn gracefully and in the right order

Calligrapher awaits inspiration

DROP BY DROP
This Ming bronze water dropper is in the shape of a boy riding a buffalo. A water dropper was used for wetting the inkstone. It was important to control the supply of water mixed with an ink stick because this affected the tone of the ink. A Tang landscape painter noted that "five colours can be obtained from black ink alone". Calligraphers and painters often had assistants to help prepare ink while they were working.

Seal

Impression

Seal-paste box, 19th century

BOLD AND BRILLIANT
This is an example of the elegant "slender gold" calligraphy of the Song emperor Hui Zong. For a calligrapher, style was as important as accuracy.

PRACTICE MAKES PERFECT
To become a good calligrapher requires years of practice. Because Chinese writing is based on signs rather than sounds, every sign, or character, must be learned by heart. The strokes that make up each character must be written in the correct sequence. With over 40,000 characters in the Chinese language, the calligrapher's art is not an easy one.

A GOOD IMPRESSION
Many scholars used a seal as a way of identifying their work. A seal would identify its owner either directly by name or with a favourite quotation. Seal impressions were always printed in red ink. Special paintings might end up covered with different impressions as later admirers and owners affixed their seals to the work.

NATURAL BEAUTY
This stoneware brush washer from the 18th century is made in the form of a lotus pod. Scholars were uplifted by the beauty of natural forms.

Brush rest in the shape of a three-peaked mountain

CELESTIAL INSPIRATION
The production of ornamental ink cakes became a minor art form. This octagonal ink cake is decorated with a celestial horse carrying sacred Daoist writings. It was made in 1621 by a famous Ming ink-cake manufacturer called Cheng Dayue. By the time of the Ming dynasty, all educated Chinese people felt they should be skilled in the art of either calligraphy or painting.

PAUSE FOR THOUGHT
A brush rest was an essential item for a calligrapher or painter. This dainty enamel brush rest would have been placed on a writing table. A calligrapher may have placed his writing brush upon it while he awaited inspiration.

Continued on next page

The poetry of landscapes

The soft inks and delicate brushstrokes used in calligraphy were also applied to painting. In the Song dynasty, this technique was used to great effect in the painting of landscapes. Inks created moody, evocative images. For "wet" works that depicted rolling mists or stormy clouds, artists brushed ink washes on to special absorbent paper. The Song emperor Hui Zong added painting to the subjects set in the top civil service examinations. The examination question quoted a line of poetry that had to be illustrated in an original way. Scholars often joined together to demonstrate the three artistic "perfections". One might paint a scene, and another would add a line of poetry in stylish calligraphy.

OFFICIAL POETS
The Song official Su Shi, right, was a famous poet. Many officials were accomplished writers of poetry and prose. Those that studied together were often posted to opposite ends of the empire, but they continued to exchange calligraphy and verse. Their correspondence counts for a great mass of Chinese literature.

The brush tip contains several different layers of hair

The inner core of hairs is often waxed to make the brush tip springy

AN EMPEROR'S POEM
This delicate jade bowl stand is carved in the shape of a *bi*, a disc used in ancient rituals. It is inscribed with a poem by the Manchu, or Qing emperor Qianlong. In the inscription, the emperor says that his "poetic imagination" was stirred by the "subtle and exquisite" shape of the bowl stand and the quality of the jade from which it is made. The foreign emperor Qianlong was a great admirer of Chinese art and collected poems, paintings, and calligraphy from the length and breadth of his empire.

High-quality jade

Goat hair tip

Buffalo horn handle

Carved dragon curls around the pot

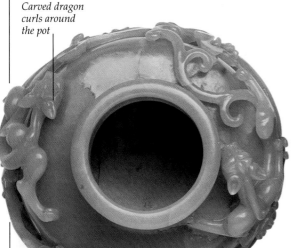

Pine tree

Modern Chinese calligraphy brushes for writing large characters

A JADE BRUSH WASHER
The feeling of harmony inspired by classical forms and designs was important to the Chinese scholar. Even the humblest objects in a scholar's studio were lovely to look at. This exquisite jade pot was actually used for washing brushes! It is carved with dragons, a favourite Chinese motif, and dates from the Ming dynasty.

Scholar deep in thought

A TRANQUIL SETTING
The scene carved on this 17th-century bamboo brush pot represents a Chinese ideal – a scholar seated quietly underneath a pine tree admiring the beauty of nature.

NATURAL HARMONY

The Song painter Guo Xi believed the main duty of the landscape painter was to bring the peace of nature into every home. A Song landscape painting usually portrayed a tranquil view of mountains and water. Guo Xi said: "When you are planning to paint, you must always create a harmonious relationship between Heaven and Earth."

"Fishing in a mountain stream" by Xu Daoning, ink on silk, 11th century

Wolf hair tip

Bamboo handle

The blue pigment was applied before the glaze

This delicate pattern was painted with a fine brush

THE PERFECT PATTERN

Like all the equipment used by a calligrapher or a painter, this pretty ceramic brush rest is elaborately decorated. The blue pattern is an example of the famous "blue and white" pottery that was first perfected in the Ming dynasty. This brush rest is probably from the late Ming period.

CAPTURED IN BRONZE

This ornate bronze brush rest resembles a classical landscape. It is cast in the shape of a five-peaked mountain range and decorated with plants and animals. The wider central spaces are for holding large brushes.

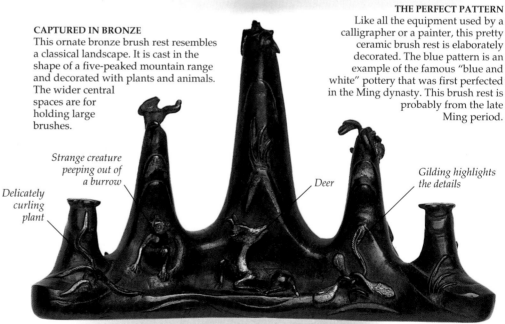

Strange creature peeping out of a burrow

Delicately curling plant

Deer

Gilding highlights the details

DIFFERENT STROKES

A painter or a calligrapher would have a large collection of brushes. Any number of brushes might be required for a landscape painting – large ones for applying a background wash and small ones for picking out detail. A professional calligrapher might need a brush with hair over half a metre long for writing big characters on banners and posters. Brushes were carefully made for these purposes. The hairs of a brush tip could be constructed to produce a soft wash, a firm and even stroke, or a lively, flamboyant line.

Life in the fields

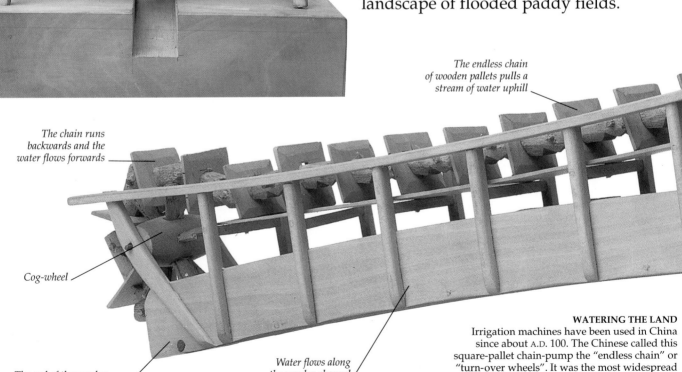

Chinese painting of the endless chain

MOST PEOPLE IN IMPERIAL CHINA lived in the countryside and worked in the fields. The hard work of the rural population formed the foundation of the great Chinese empire. The majority of peasant farmers lived on carefully tended, family-owned plots of land. Although they were not tied to any lord, they had to pay taxes, serve in the army, and work for a certain number of days a year on public works such as roads and canals. After the great peasant rebellion that toppled the Qin dynasty in 207 B.C., most emperors were careful not to overburden their rural subjects. All the same, the life of a peasant farmer was hard. Most farm jobs were carried out by hand, from hoeing the ground to spreading manure. One of the main tasks of a farmer and his family was to maintain a regular supply of water to the crops. They transported water by bucket or used irrigation machines that were manually operated. In the hills of northern China, crops were planted on narrow terraces carved into the hillsides. Water was raised to the terraces from wells and canals by human-powered irrigation machines. In the rice growing regions of southern China, the well-organized irrigation systems created a patchwork landscape of flooded paddy fields.

Workers chatted to wile away the long hours

The men balanced on a wooden bar

The endless chain of wooden pallets pulls a stream of water uphill

The chain runs backwards and the water flows forwards

Cog-wheel

The end of the wooden channel rests in a stream or canal

Water flows along the wooden channel

WATERING THE LAND
Irrigation machines have been used in China since about A.D. 100. The Chinese called this square-pallet chain-pump the "endless chain" or "turn-over wheels". It was the most widespread kind of irrigation machine used in the Chinese empire. The pump raised water from irrigation ditches and streams into channels that surrounded the fields. Two people working this machine could irrigate hundreds of plots of land.

Hair worn in a traditional topknot

The heads of the workers were often protected from the sun by a small roof (shown in the painting opposite)

FOOD FOR AN EMPIRE
The mountainous terrain of northern China is covered with a rich, yellow soil called loess, which was originally blown in from the Mongolian desert. Chinese farmers cut terraces into the hillsides to make the most of this fertile land. They grew millet and wheat in the long, narrow fields that wound around the hillsides. In southern China, farmers grew rice in the well-irrigated valleys of the Yangzi River. From the Tang dynasty onwards, the bulk of the empire's food was grown here.

Threshing

Winnowing

Transporting the grain

The pedals turn a large cog-wheel, which pulls the chain of square wooden pallets

Cog-wheel turns backwards

THE COST OF FAILURE
Every member of a peasant family had to work hard on the farm, particularly at harvest time. Many peasant farmers had to give a large share of their harvest to a wealthy landlord, as well as pay tax to the emperor. If the crops failed, a peasant family was in danger of falling into debt and losing its land.

Water runs out of the channel into an irrigation ditch on a higher level

Continued on next page

Seeds and ploughshares

Traditionally peasant farmers used ancient methods of farming which involved hoeing their crops by hand, transporting water by bucket, and grinding grain with manually operated mills. In the Han dynasty, wealthy farmers built bigger, labour-saving machines powered by water or animals. Iron ploughshares pulled by oxen, new irrigation machines, and watermills greatly improved farming output. However, small farmers still relied on human labour. By the Song dynasty, new crop strains and knowledge of fertilizers allowed the peasant farmers in southern China to grow two crops a year in the same field.

REMOVING THE HUSKS
This hand-powered winnowing machine was used to separate the outer shells, or husks, from the grain. Winnowing was traditionally carried out by shaking the grain in a large sieve, then tossing it in the air to remove the husks.

THE HUMAN HAMMER
Harvested grain was crushed by a tilt-hammer. This machine was powered by a single man who used his weight to tilt the hammer backwards and forwards in a see-saw action. There were larger, water-driven tilt-hammers in mills near towns and cities.

PLANTING OUT A PADDY FIELD
These peasant farmers are transplanting young rice plants in the soft mud of a paddy field. Originally rice was grown only in flooded paddies, but later farmers cultivated rice in dry fields in areas supplied with a good rainfall.

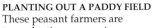

ALL HANDS TO THE HARVEST
This painting from the Yuan dynasty shows a group of peasant farmers harvesting rice. In rural communities, everyone helped with the farm work and women laboured alongside men in the fields. Peasant women never had their feet bound because they would have been unable to carry out any kind of field work.

PLOUGHING THE LAND
During the Han dynasty, government iron foundries began producing ploughshares. They were made in various sizes, from large ploughshares that were pulled by an oxen team to small, pointed ones that could be used by a single person. According to an ancient Chinese proverb, farmers should always plough their land after rain to conserve the moisture in the ground. The new iron equipment made this back-breaking task much easier.

Hoe

Plough

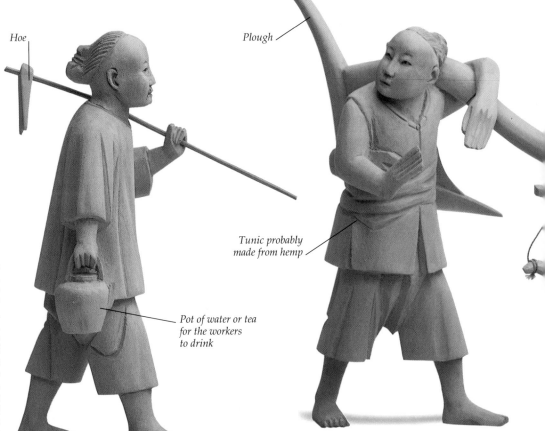

Tunic probably made from hemp

A LITTLE HELP FROM SOME FRIENDS
This 19th-century model depicts a group of peasant farmers going off to plough their fields. Although every rural family had to support itself, co-operation with friends and neighbours was essential. The upkeep of irrigation ditches and the repair of terraces were tasks shared by the whole village. Larger enterprises were organized by local government. In 111 B.C., the Han emperor Wu Di said: "Agriculture is the basic occupation of the world. So the imperial government must cut canals and ditches, guide the rivers, and build reservoirs in order to prevent flood and drought."

Pot of water or tea for the workers to drink

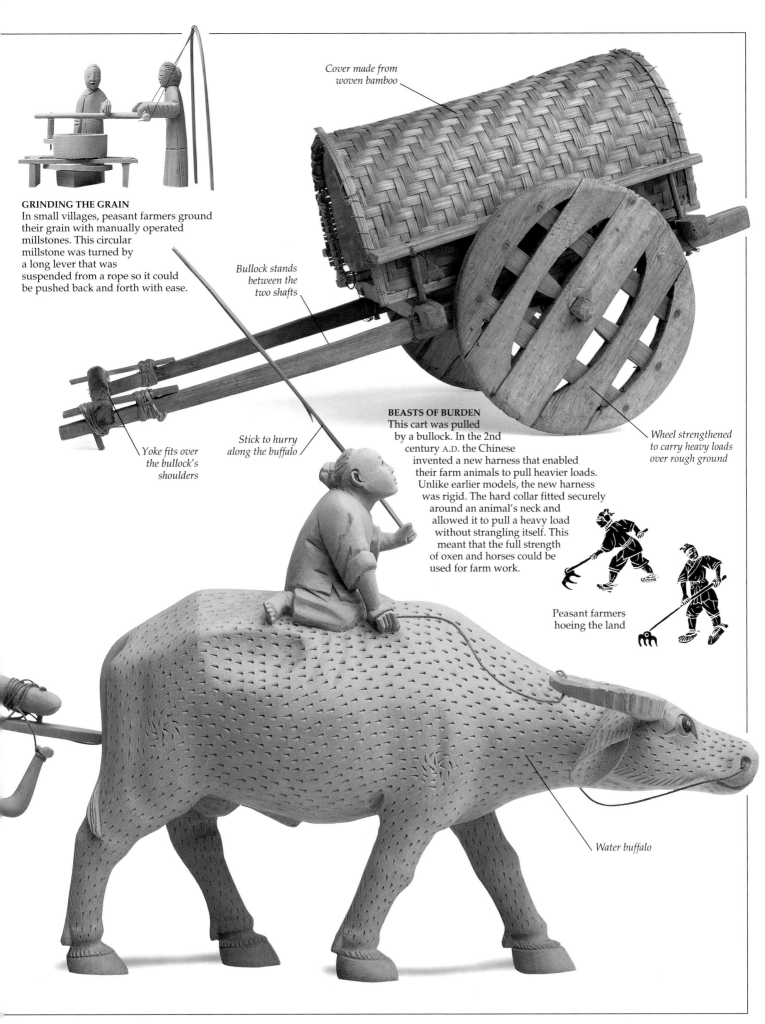

GRINDING THE GRAIN
In small villages, peasant farmers ground their grain with manually operated millstones. This circular millstone was turned by a long lever that was suspended from a rope so it could be pushed back and forth with ease.

Cover made from woven bamboo

Bullock stands between the two shafts

Yoke fits over the bullock's shoulders

Stick to hurry along the buffalo

Wheel strengthened to carry heavy loads over rough ground

BEASTS OF BURDEN
This cart was pulled by a bullock. In the 2nd century A.D. the Chinese invented a new harness that enabled their farm animals to pull heavier loads. Unlike earlier models, the new harness was rigid. The hard collar fitted securely around an animal's neck and allowed it to pull a heavy load without strangling itself. This meant that the full strength of oxen and horses could be used for farm work.

Peasant farmers hoeing the land

Water buffalo

Great waterways

CHINA IS DOMINATED BY TWO GREAT RIVERS, the Yellow River in northern China and the Yangzi in the south. The Yellow River flows through rich loess soil which is deposited over its surrounding plains. The first civilization in China grew up in these fertile lands. Over the centuries, the Yellow River often broke its banks and caused devastating floods. This tendency to flood led to the river's other name: "China's sorrow". The Yangzi River provided a water supply for rice cultivation in the warm southern climate, and its rich delta became China's main rice growing region. In the 6th century, the Yellow and Yangzi rivers were linked by the Grand Canal, a great waterway that stretched across the Chinese empire. The canal was used to transport rice from the Yangzi delta to northern China, where the imperial capital was situated.

A STRONG ELEMENT
According to ancient Chinese philosophy, there were two natural forces – the yin and the yang. In nature, these forces existed in a delicate state of balance. The Chinese believed the disruption of this balance by humans caused natural disasters such as floods. Therefore, Chinese engineers were careful not to disturb the natural courses of rivers. In the painting above a boy is being taught about the yin and the yang, which are symbolized by the circular sign on the scroll.

Powerful beak for catching fish

Long, snaky neck stretches out under water

Cormorants

URBAN WATERWAYS
Many cities in southern China were built on networks of canals. These busy urban waterways were crowded with junks and sampans. Some families made their homes on boats, rafts, or barges and spent their whole lives afloat. Water taxis ferried passengers from one part of the city to another, while wealthy people often travelled along city canals in their own splendidly decorated boats.

19th-century model ferry boat, or water taxi

The oar is operated by moving it from side to side

Eye for the boat to see with

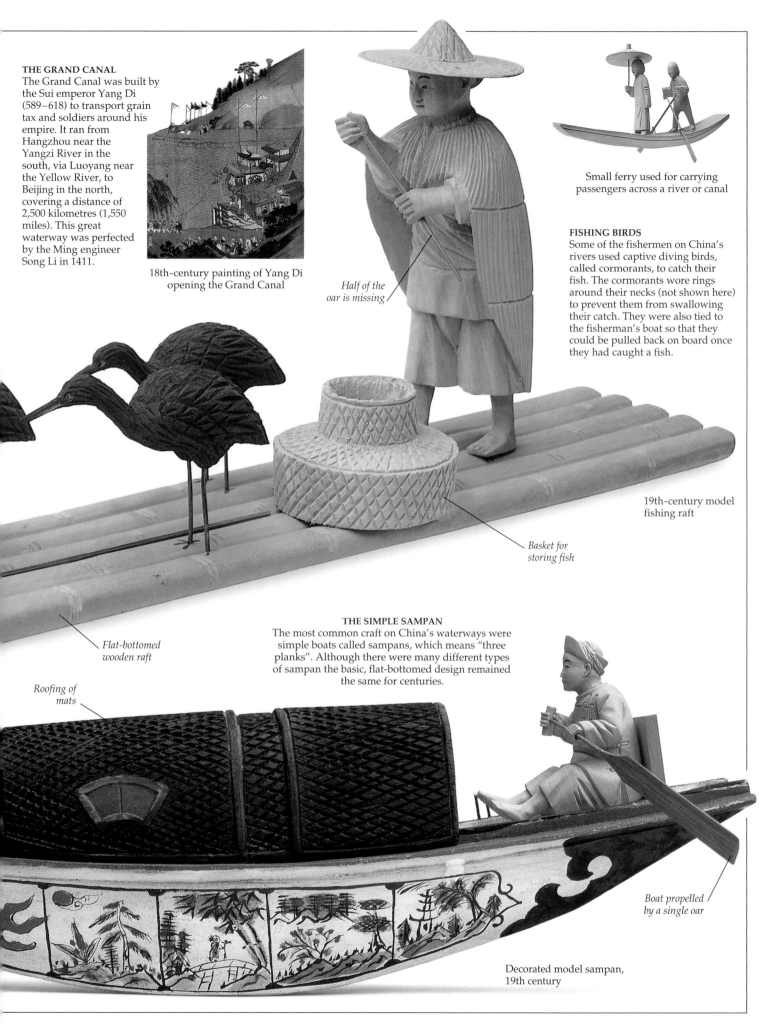

THE GRAND CANAL
The Grand Canal was built by the Sui emperor Yang Di (589–618) to transport grain tax and soldiers around his empire. It ran from Hangzhou near the Yangzi River in the south, via Luoyang near the Yellow River, to Beijing in the north, covering a distance of 2,500 kilometres (1,550 miles). This great waterway was perfected by the Ming engineer Song Li in 1411.

18th-century painting of Yang Di opening the Grand Canal

Small ferry used for carrying passengers across a river or canal

FISHING BIRDS
Some of the fishermen on China's rivers used captive diving birds, called cormorants, to catch their fish. The cormorants wore rings around their necks (not shown here) to prevent them from swallowing their catch. They were also tied to the fisherman's boat so that they could be pulled back on board once they had caught a fish.

Half of the oar is missing

19th-century model fishing raft

Basket for storing fish

Flat-bottomed wooden raft

THE SIMPLE SAMPAN
The most common craft on China's waterways were simple boats called sampans, which means "three planks". Although there were many different types of sampan the basic, flat-bottomed design remained the same for centuries.

Roofing of mats

Boat propelled by a single oar

Decorated model sampan, 19th century

Within the city walls

Circular end-tile

Lookout

KEEPING A LOOK-OUT
This pottery model of a watchtower dates from the Han dynasty. Watchtowers were common in Chinese towns and cities because the authorities kept a strict eye on the inhabitants.

Tʜᴇ ʟᴀɴᴅꜱᴄᴀᴘᴇ ᴏꜰ ɪᴍᴘᴇʀɪᴀʟ Cʜɪɴᴀ was dotted with walled towns and cities. These enclosed urban communities were centres of government and the power of the authorities was reinforced by town planning. Towns and cities were traditionally built on a grid system and divided into sections called wards. Each ward was surrounded by walls with gates that were locked every evening. Drums sounded from a central tower to warn inhabitants when the gates were closing, and often visiting friends or relatives would have to stay overnight. In general, wealthy people and government officials lived at one end of a town or city and the poor at the other. Markets were usually situated along one of the main streets. In the later years of the Chinese empire, towns and cities were built on a less rigid structure. However, citizens were always firmly under the control of the authorities. A French resident of 18th-century Beijing reported: "The police know all that is going on, even inside the palaces of the princes. They keep exact registers of the inhabitants of every house."

COUNTING THE COST
Towns and cities were centres of trade and commerce. Local peasant farmers brought their produce to market and also their grain-tax to be collected by officials. Large transactions may have been carried out with the aid of an abacus such as this one. The exact origin of this helpful calculating device is unknown, but it was certainly in common use by the Ming dynasty.

ON THE TILES
Traditional Chinese buildings were protected by heavy, overhanging tile roofs. In Chinese belief, a roof was a safeguard against bad spirits as well as harsh weather. Roof tiles were often decorated with symbols and inscriptions to ward off evil influences.

The dragon is a good luck symbol

Pottery roof tiles, Ming dynasty

DRUMMING UP TRADE
This pellet-drum was used to attract customers. Street vendors had their own sounds to announce their presence and advertise their wares.

Cup for ladling out food

STREET TRADE
This man is selling food. Hawkers wandered the streets of every Chinese town or city selling cooked and uncooked foods. The main streets were lined with market stalls that sold all kinds of produce. People could buy special dishes from stallholders to take home for family meals.

A pellet-drum was held in the hand and twirled from side to side

Pottery roof ornament from a palace roof, Ming dynasty

ROOF GUARDIAN
This yellow pottery beast was placed at the end of a roof ridge. Mythical beasts like this were intended to act as guardians. Official buildings and the houses of wealthy people were often highly ornamented with decorated tiles and pottery figures.

Yellow roof tiles were used on important buildings

Classical pagoda

Platform

Overhanging tile roof

Traditional Chinese buildings, Ming dynasty

TRADITIONAL ARCHITECTURE
Chinese buildings were raised above the damp ground on platforms of rammed earth, brick, or stone. Their heavy, overhanging roofs were supported by a structure of sturdy wooden beams, which allowed for movement in an earthquake.

CITY WALL
This European engraving shows the strong walls surrounding a city. Traditionally the walls of towns and cities were built in a square shape, which symbolized the four corners of the Earth. It was important for the Chinese to feel that they were in tune with nature. The site for a new town or city was carefully chosen using cosmological calculations to make sure that its position was a favourable one.

Pottery roof tiles, Ming dynasty

At home

In most Chinese homes, three generations of the same family lived under one roof. Families followed strict codes of conduct, which were reflected in the layout of their houses. A traditional home was divided into different sections by courtyards. The main gate led into an outer courtyard in which traders were received. Rooms along the sides of the outer courtyard were used for housing guests, and they often contained a library as well. An inner courtyard was reserved for the family. The head of the household, usually the grandfather, lived with his wife and children in the main building, with side rooms allocated to close relatives. Behind the main building were the kitchens and rooms for servants. Some houses were surrounded by gardens, which were enclosed within an outer wall.

Dragon head

SPECIAL ADVICE
Families used divination sticks like these to seek advice from their ancestors on family matters. They were kept with the ancestral tablets in the household shrine, where the family paid respects to their ancestors on special days of the year.

The phoenix, or fong, is a mythical bird that symbolizes good luck

Detail from pillow decoration

SIMPLE COMFORTS
Poorer Chinese people lived simply in their homes. They slept on rush mats and rested their heads on pillows made from wood or pottery.

Pottery pillow, 12th–13th century

Stoneware pillow, 12th–13th century

Son kneels before his father

PAYING RESPECTS
Family life in China was governed by strict rules. Confucius taught that children should respect and obey their parents, and it was written in law that a wife must be obedient to her husband. Although this sounds harsh, most Chinese families shared mutual affection and respect. This 12th-century painting shows a son, along with his wife and family, paying respects to his father.

Detail from pillow decoration

Weeping bride

LOSING A DAUGHTER
The painting on this pillow probably depicts a wedding procession. The bride is weeping because she was expected to shed tears of sorrow on leaving her own family and tears of joy on joining the family of her husband. A single girl had to obey her father, but when she married, she had to obey her husband and her new parents-in-law.

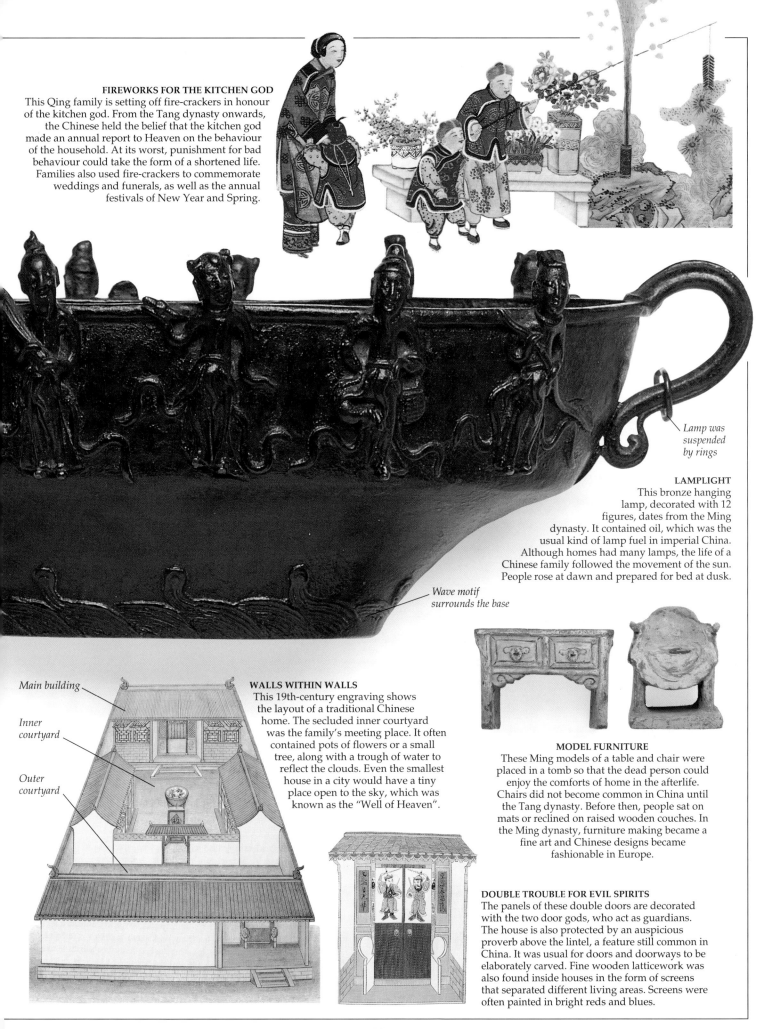

FIREWORKS FOR THE KITCHEN GOD
This Qing family is setting off fire-crackers in honour of the kitchen god. From the Tang dynasty onwards, the Chinese held the belief that the kitchen god made an annual report to Heaven on the behaviour of the household. At its worst, punishment for bad behaviour could take the form of a shortened life. Families also used fire-crackers to commemorate weddings and funerals, as well as the annual festivals of New Year and Spring.

Lamp was suspended by rings

LAMPLIGHT
This bronze hanging lamp, decorated with 12 figures, dates from the Ming dynasty. It contained oil, which was the usual kind of lamp fuel in imperial China. Although homes had many lamps, the life of a Chinese family followed the movement of the sun. People rose at dawn and prepared for bed at dusk.

Wave motif surrounds the base

Main building

Inner courtyard

Outer courtyard

WALLS WITHIN WALLS
This 19th-century engraving shows the layout of a traditional Chinese home. The secluded inner courtyard was the family's meeting place. It often contained pots of flowers or a small tree, along with a trough of water to reflect the clouds. Even the smallest house in a city would have a tiny place open to the sky, which was known as the "Well of Heaven".

MODEL FURNITURE
These Ming models of a table and chair were placed in a tomb so that the dead person could enjoy the comforts of home in the afterlife. Chairs did not become common in China until the Tang dynasty. Before then, people sat on mats or reclined on raised wooden couches. In the Ming dynasty, furniture making became a fine art and Chinese designs became fashionable in Europe.

DOUBLE TROUBLE FOR EVIL SPIRITS
The panels of these double doors are decorated with the two door gods, who act as guardians. The house is also protected by an auspicious proverb above the lintel, a feature still common in China. It was usual for doors and doorways to be elaborately carved. Fine wooden latticework was also found inside houses in the form of screens that separated different living areas. Screens were often painted in bright reds and blues.

Food and drink

Court ladies enjoying a banquet, Tang dynasty

IN CHINA, THE ART OF COOKING has been celebrated since early times. Feasts formed an important part of Chinese life and wealthy people often enjoyed elaborate banquets. In contrast, for most of the year ordinary people lived on a simple diet of pulses and vegetables, with very little meat. Though rice was always the favourite staple food in China, people in the northern provinces ate mainly millet and some wheat. Both rich and poor Chinese flavoured their food with a wide variety of herbs and spices. To save fuel, food was chopped into small pieces and cooked quickly in an iron frying pan, or *wok*, for a few minutes only. Many foods were also steamed or stewed. Today Chinese food is enjoyed throughout the world.

A sharp knife, the main tool of a Chinese cook

Chopsticks

Case for chopstick and knife set

TEA CONNOISSEURS
Tea, or *cha*, has been grown in China since the 2nd century B.C. By the Tang dynasty, tea-making had become a fine art. These Yuan-dynasty tea merchants are taking part in a tea-tasting competition. As experts, they would be able to tell apart the many delicately flavoured varieties of Chinese tea.

NATURALLY PRESERVED
The Chinese preserved much of their food by drying it in the sun, and dried ingredients are common in Chinese cookery. After soaking in cold water, this dried cuttlefish can be used to flavour a stir-fried dish.

Song-dynasty tea bowls, 12th century

TIME FOR TEA
The Chinese drank tea from teabowls, which rested on lacquer bowl stands. Before the 12th century, hot water was boiled in water ewers and poured on to powdered tea in bowls. In the 13th century, people began to steep loose tea leaves in hot water, and the teapot came into use. Today, there are six main kinds of Chinese tea: red, black, green, Wuloong, flower, and brick. Brick tea is a mixture of teas pressed into a block. The tea shown on the right is called "gunpowder" tea because its leaves are rolled into tiny balls that resemble lead shot.

Tea leaves unfurl when soaked in water

Peanuts, eaten as a tasty snack or added to cooked dishes

CHOPSTICKS
In China, food is sliced into thin slivers before cooking, so people do not need to use knives to cut up their food when they are eating. Instead, the Chinese use chopsticks to pick up morsels of food from small porcelain bowls.

Porcelain bowl, 18th century

Peas, often ground into flour

A china bowl preserves the taste of food

Mung beans, eaten as a sweet or a savoury

Soya beans, processed into curd, milk, dried sticks, or soya sauce

Wheat, often used to make dumplings

Soya bean curd, or *doufu* (tofu), can be steamed, boiled, or fried

Rice, used to make wine as well as cakes and puddings

A STAPLE DIET
Rice was grown mainly in the southern Chinese provinces, but with improved transportation, it became the favourite staple food throughout China. Millet and wheat were the chief crops grown in the north, but wheat never formed a staple part of the Chinese diet as it did in Europe and America. Beans were an important source of protein for the Chinese – soya beans contain more protein than any other plant or animal food.

THE SPICE OF LIFE
The Chinese have always relished different tastes and flavours. Chinese cooks became expert at blending herbs and spices to create sweet, sour, bitter, hot, or salty tastes. Seasoning was important to ordinary people because much of their basic diet consisted of quite bland food. Soya beans were fermented to make tasty soya sauce, and more delicate flavours were derived from ingredients such as flower petals and tangerine peel.

Star aniseed, a popular spice native to China

Chili peppers, traditionally added to hot, spicy dishes in south-western China

Ginger, originally used to disguise the odour of old meat

Noodles, made from wheat, bean, or rice flour

Sesame seeds, sprinkled on both sweet and savoury foods

Dressed for best

THE CLOTHES OF RICH AND POOR Chinese were very different. Peasant farmers wore loose garments made usually of hemp, a rough fabric woven from plant fibres. Members of the imperial court, wealthy ladies, high-ranking officials, and scholars wore splendid robes of fine silk. This luxurious material was reserved exclusively for the use of these privileged groups. In some dynasties, rich merchants who traded in silk were forbidden from wearing it themselves, and many were punished for wearing fine silk beneath their outer garments. The supply of materials used for making clothes was protected by imperial decree. Both hemp and silk cloth were stockpiled in government storehouses in case of shortages. Towards the end of the empire, cotton became popular, but it never replaced silk as a luxury fabric.

PERSONAL GROOMING
Beauty treatment was always a matter of concern for the well-born Chinese lady. The eyebrows received special attention. They were plucked with tweezers and were usually enhanced by painting as well.

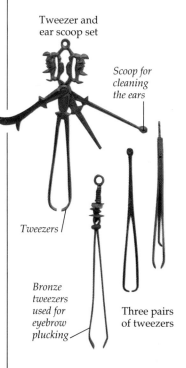

Tweezer and ear scoop set

Scoop for cleaning the ears

Tweezers

Bronze tweezers used for eyebrow plucking

Three pairs of tweezers

Luxurious vermilion-coloured silk

Scoop

Jade ear scoop

Tongue scraper

Silk tassels

SILK TIES
These red silk ankle bands were used for binding on gaiters. The richness of the embroidery shows that they came from the wardrobe of a wealthy lady. Embroidery was common on clothes worn by both men and women of quality. Designs often included good luck symbols or mythological scenes.

The peony, often called the "king of flowers" because of its large red petals, was a popular decorative motif

The outer segment of the fan is decorated with a garden scene

CARVED IVORY FAN
Fans were a favourite item of dress for both men and women in China. This expensive ivory fan is decorated with intricately carved flowers and trees. Cheaper fans were made from bamboo and paper. Their decoration could take the form of a painting or a poem.

Delicate flowers embroidered in silk thread

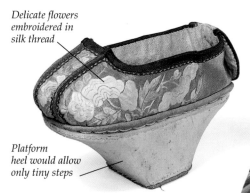

Platform heel would allow only tiny steps

PLATFORM SHOE
This delicate platform slipper belonged to a Manchu lady. The Manchus ruled China during the Qing dynasty. Unlike wealthy Chinese women, Manchu women did not bind their feet to make them smaller. The Chinese believed that tiny, pointed feet were an essential feature of female beauty, and girls' feet were bound from early childhood. As late as 1902, a Manchu emperor issued an order banning this painful practice.

Fine silk cloth is light to wear

Wide sleeve

Miniature roundel, or circular design

Silk toggle used to fasten the robe

The butterfly is a symbol of joy

The yellow lotus is a sacred Chinese flower

FLOWING SILK ROBE
The beauty of this 19th-century silk robe indicates that it was once worn by a lady of considerable taste. It is made from a kind of silk tapestry called *kesi* in which the pattern is woven into the fabric. The wonderful design of flowers and butterflies is intended to create the impression of spring. Along the hem, the garment is finished with a traditional wave border.

An elaborate roundel, a design popular towards the end of the empire

The bat is an emblem of good luck

The peony represents spring

Wave border

Festivals and games

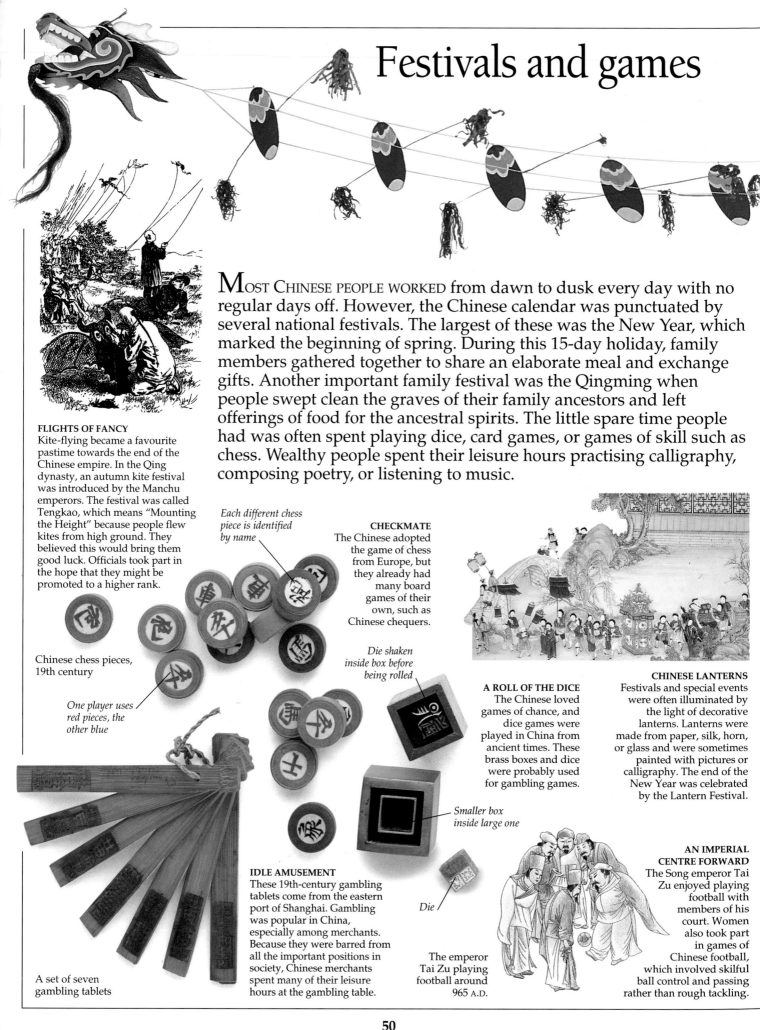

MOST CHINESE PEOPLE WORKED from dawn to dusk every day with no regular days off. However, the Chinese calendar was punctuated by several national festivals. The largest of these was the New Year, which marked the beginning of spring. During this 15-day holiday, family members gathered together to share an elaborate meal and exchange gifts. Another important family festival was the Qingming when people swept clean the graves of their family ancestors and left offerings of food for the ancestral spirits. The little spare time people had was often spent playing dice, card games, or games of skill such as chess. Wealthy people spent their leisure hours practising calligraphy, composing poetry, or listening to music.

FLIGHTS OF FANCY
Kite-flying became a favourite pastime towards the end of the Chinese empire. In the Qing dynasty, an autumn kite festival was introduced by the Manchu emperors. The festival was called Tengkao, which means "Mounting the Height" because people flew kites from high ground. They believed this would bring them good luck. Officials took part in the hope that they might be promoted to a higher rank.

Each different chess piece is identified by name

CHECKMATE
The Chinese adopted the game of chess from Europe, but they already had many board games of their own, such as Chinese chequers.

Chinese chess pieces, 19th century

One player uses red pieces, the other blue

Die shaken inside box before being rolled

A ROLL OF THE DICE
The Chinese loved games of chance, and dice games were played in China from ancient times. These brass boxes and dice were probably used for gambling games.

CHINESE LANTERNS
Festivals and special events were often illuminated by the light of decorative lanterns. Lanterns were made from paper, silk, horn, or glass and were sometimes painted with pictures or calligraphy. The end of the New Year was celebrated by the Lantern Festival.

Smaller box inside large one

IDLE AMUSEMENT
These 19th-century gambling tablets come from the eastern port of Shanghai. Gambling was popular in China, especially among merchants. Because they were barred from all the important positions in society, Chinese merchants spent many of their leisure hours at the gambling table.

Die

A set of seven gambling tablets

The emperor Tai Zu playing football around 965 A.D.

AN IMPERIAL CENTRE FORWARD
The Song emperor Tai Zu enjoyed playing football with members of his court. Women also took part in games of Chinese football, which involved skilful ball control and passing rather than rough tackling.

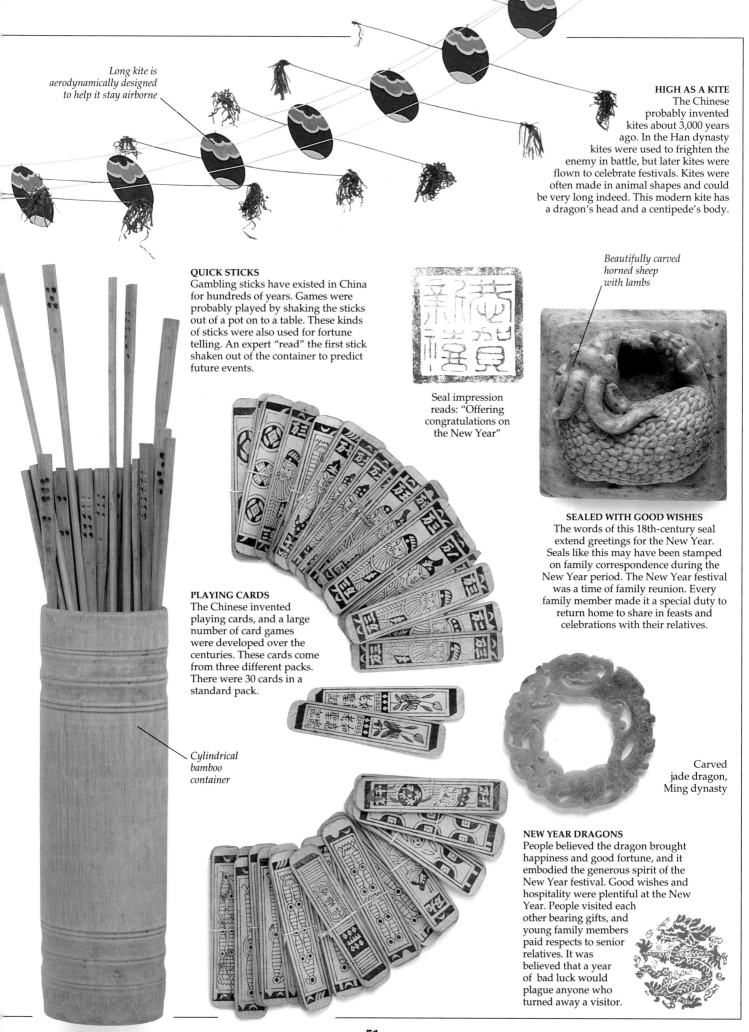

Long kite is aerodynamically designed to help it stay airborne

HIGH AS A KITE
The Chinese probably invented kites about 3,000 years ago. In the Han dynasty kites were used to frighten the enemy in battle, but later kites were flown to celebrate festivals. Kites were often made in animal shapes and could be very long indeed. This modern kite has a dragon's head and a centipede's body.

QUICK STICKS
Gambling sticks have existed in China for hundreds of years. Games were probably played by shaking the sticks out of a pot on to a table. These kinds of sticks were also used for fortune telling. An expert "read" the first stick shaken out of the container to predict future events.

Beautifully carved horned sheep with lambs

Seal impression reads: "Offering congratulations on the New Year"

SEALED WITH GOOD WISHES
The words of this 18th-century seal extend greetings for the New Year. Seals like this may have been stamped on family correspondence during the New Year period. The New Year festival was a time of family reunion. Every family member made it a special duty to return home to share in feasts and celebrations with their relatives.

PLAYING CARDS
The Chinese invented playing cards, and a large number of card games were developed over the centuries. These cards come from three different packs. There were 30 cards in a standard pack.

Cylindrical bamboo container

Carved jade dragon, Ming dynasty

NEW YEAR DRAGONS
People believed the dragon brought happiness and good fortune, and it embodied the generous spirit of the New Year festival. Good wishes and hospitality were plentiful at the New Year. People visited each other bearing gifts, and young family members paid respects to senior relatives. It was believed that a year of bad luck would plague anyone who turned away a visitor.

Living in harmony

IN IMPERIAL CHINA, MUSIC was thought to be an important part of civilized life. At the royal palace, the court orchestra played when the emperor received visitors or held banquets. Beautiful ceremonial music also accompanied religious rituals. Confucius thought music was almost as necessary as food. He believed that playing an instrument, singing, or listening to a suitable musical composition encouraged a sense of inner harmony. On the other hand, he thought that certain kinds of music led to rowdy or violent behaviour, and he condemned these as immoral. As an unknown scholar remarked: "The greatest music is that filled with the most delicate sounds."

HISTORY IN SONG
In later imperial China, opera was the most popular form of theatre. Operas usually related stories based on great historical events, often with a great deal of humour mixed in. Characters were identified by their vividly painted faces. Traditional Chinese opera is still performed. The scene above is from a production in Shanghai.

Assembled *sheng*

Band to hold pipes together

The *sheng*, seen here in pieces, is made up of 17 pipes

Wind chamber and mouth-piece seen from above

Mouthpiece

Brass "reeds" create the sound

Finger holes

AN ANCIENT MOUTH-ORGAN
The *sheng* is a Chinese mouth organ made from bamboo pipes. It is played by blowing into and sucking air from a wind chamber while fingering the holes in the pipes. Several *sheng* were played together. This kind of wind instrument has been in existence in China since ancient times.

MUSIC IN THE AFTERLIFE
Since music was considered such an important part of life, models of musicians were often placed in tombs to provide entertainment in the afterlife. This little terracotta orchestra, complete with a dancing girl, was found in a Tang-dynasty tomb. The figures were once painted with bright colours.

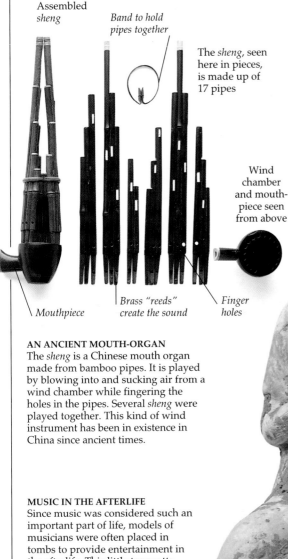

Harp

Strings would have been threaded into model

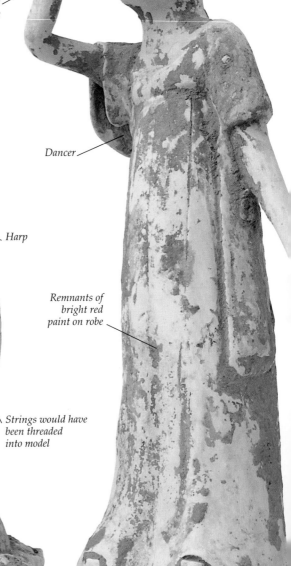

Long, elegant sleeve

Dancer

Remnants of bright red paint on robe

MANY STRINGS ATTACHED
The *yang qin*, or "foreign zither", was a late addition to the Chinese orchestra. It was introduced into China in about the 18th century and soon became popular. The *yang qin* is played by striking the strings with a pair of delicate beaters. Its 14 strings produce a wide range of silvery notes.

Bridge

Perforations let sound out of box

Wooden beaters

Tuning tool

Tuning pegs

Lacquered board

Bridge

19th-century *qin*

Strings are plucked by hand

Mother-of-pearl discs indicate finger positions

THE LYRICAL LUTE
The classical lute, or *qin*, is a kind of Chinese zither with seven strings. The *qin* dates back over 2,000 years, and older designs had up to 20 strings. The music of the *qin* was greatly admired for its gentle, plaintive quality and it was a favourite instrument in imperial China.

Remnants of blue paint on headdress

Flute

Lute

COURT ORCHESTRA
Many court occasions were accompanied by music. These female musicians are playing various wind and string instruments including the *sheng*, the flute, and the *qin*. The musician in the bottom right-hand corner is playing another popular Chinese instrument, the drum.

Gardens of Heaven

THE CHINESE LOOKED ON GARDENS as works of art. The main elements of a garden were the same as those of a traditional landscape painting – craggy mountains and still water. These appeared in gardens as outcrops of weatherworn rock and tranquil lakes or ponds. Chinese gardens were designed to reflect nature in other ways. Trees were allowed to grow into interesting gnarled shapes, and plants and flowers were cultivated in natural-looking clumps. The garden was a place for quiet thought and spiritual refreshment. Unexpected features that inspired the imagination were prized, and graceful pavilions and bridges enhanced the impression of natural harmony. Towns and cities were planned to include secluded parks where, as a Ming garden treatise promised, the urban population could find "stillness in the midst of the city turmoil".

NATURE PERFECTED
The natural arrangement of the Chinese garden can be seen in this 19th-century painting of the palace gardens in Beijing. Visitors to these famous landscape gardens felt they were entering a natural paradise. Artificial hills and lakes, bright flowers, elegant pines, and ornamental rocks were creatively assembled to reflect the glories of nature.

Detail from purse decoration

With its sweet song, the cicada was a welcome visitor to the Chinese garden

Lotus-shaped cup carved from horn

SACRED BLOSSOMS
The lotus was regarded as the supreme flower of summer. Its pale blossoms graced the tranquil lakes and pools of many Chinese parks and gardens. The lotus was seen as a symbol of purity and was sacred to both the Buddhist and Daoist religions.

KING OF FLOWERS
The peony symbolized spring. It was known as the "king of flowers" because of its large, red petals. Chinese gardeners planted peonies in dense clumps or along walls.

The bright, dancing butterfly was a symbol of joy

Swallowtail butterfly

Peony

NATURE STUDY
This 19th-century purse is beautifully embroidered with a butterfly and a cicada. The Chinese had great respect for such tiny creatures, because Buddhism taught that every living thing had a special value. Gardens were an ideal place for the study of nature. The Song emperor Hui Zong held competitions in the painting of flowers, birds, and insects in the lovely palace gardens of Kaifeng.

THE KINGDOM OF FLOWERS
The Chinese loved flowers, as the floral motif of this embroidered sleeve band shows. China was known as the "Flowery Kingdom". It is the original home of many flowers, trees, and fruits now grown throughout the world. The orange, the tea rose, the plane tree, the rhododendron, and the Chinese gooseberry, which is commonly known as the kiwi fruit, are all native Chinese plants.

FLOWER POWER
Garden plants and flowers were prized for their symbolic value as well as for their natural beauty. The winter plum blossom, for example, symbolized personal renewal, and the tough bamboo plant stood for strength and lasting friendship. These exquisite lacquer boxes from the Ming dynasty are carved with some of China's most popular flowers, including the peony and the chrysanthemum.

NATURALLY INSPIRED
Gardens were favourite places for literary meetings. These Ming scholars have gathered together in a garden to read and write poetry. An "ink boy" prepares a supply of ink to make sure that the scholar who is about to compose verse will not have to interrupt his flow once inspiration strikes.

FLOWER OF FORTUNE
The narcissus was a favourite New Year flower. The opening of its delicate buds was thought to bring good luck for the year ahead.

Details from sleeve band decoration

A lovely butterfly attracted to fragrant garden flowers

The chrysanthemum was carefully cultivated in China

FRUIT OF PARADISE
The bright red fruit of the lychee tree adorned many gardens in southern China. This attractive fruit was also prized for its juicy white flesh.

LASTING BEAUTY
The chrysanthemum was the flower of autumn. It was esteemed for the variety and richness of its colours. Because it outlasted the frost, the chrysanthemum was adopted as the Chinese symbol for long life.

The peach is a symbol of eternal life

Arts and crafts

CHINA HAS ALWAYS BEEN RENOWNED for its exquisite arts and crafts. In imperial China, luxury goods formed the major export commodities – Chinese bronze, jade, silk, lacquer, and porcelain were prized in Asia and Europe. Although the manufacture of decorative objects involved sophisticated techniques, many were mass-produced. From the Shang dynasty onwards, Chinese rulers controlled the supply of raw materials and ran government factories. These were manned by skilled artisans who carried out the different stages of the manufacturing processes. Unlike the merchants who sold their handiwork, artisans were well thought of in China. After the scholars and the peasant farmers, artisans were considered the most important members of society. They produced tools for agriculture and weapons for the army as well as luxury items such as decorated tableware and fine silk cloth.

BEAUTIFUL BRONZE
In ancient China, bronze was made into stunning ritual vessels and weaponry. This circular fitting, which dates from Shang times, probably decorated a harness or a shield. Later, in about the 6th century B.C., the Chinese refined the process of iron casting. From then on government iron foundries produced iron and even steel in bulk.

Underside of teacup

Lead glazes run to give a swirly pattern

POTS OF STYLE
China is famous for its beautiful, high-quality ceramics. This is due partly to the rich deposits of suitable clay and porcelain stone found in China. Over the centuries Chinese craftsmen developed a wide range of innovative techniques for making and decorating ceramics. One of the most famous styles was the "blue and white" porcelain manufactured in the Ming dynasty. Large amounts of this were exported to Europe from the 15th century onwards. Another distinctive style was the "three-colour" pottery popular in the Tang dynasty. This was decorated with three colours of lead glaze to create bold, splashy patterns, as seen on the Tang teacups above.

BURNISHED GOLD
Some of China's finest pieces of art were religious or ceremonial objects. This beautiful gilt bronze figure represents the Buddha of Immeasurable Light. Chinese craftsmen often decorated the Buddha with bright, shining gold, or gilt, to emphasize his holiness.

Gold leaf or gold dust is applied to bronze to give a bright finish

Bronze Buddha, Ming dynasty

Mother-of-pearl inlay

FIT FOR A KING
This exquisite box from the Ming dynasty is made from lacquered basketry inlaid with mother-of-pearl. It is decorated with a romantic scene showing a scholar taking leave of his friends. A lacquered finish took many days to produce and was usually highly decorated. Since lacquer ware was both expensive and beautiful, it was often given as an imperial gift to neighbouring rulers. In Korea and Japan Chinese lacquer was greatly admired.

Ming cup

THE MOST PRECIOUS STONE
Jade was highly prized by the Chinese from ancient times. This lustrous gemstone occurs in soft greens, greys, and browns, and is satiny smooth when polished. The Chinese believed that jade was vested with magical properties, and it has long been associated with immortality.

The fish is a sacred Buddhist symbol that represents spiritual liberation

A vase symbolizes immortality

Enamel paste is applied to tiny metal compartments called cloisons

RAINBOW COLOURS
This lovely Qing-dynasty fish vase is decorated with cloisonné enamel. This enamelling technique was a foreign invention first produced in China in the early Ming dynasty. At first, many Chinese thought the bright colours used for cloisonné ware were vulgar, but by the 15th century cloisonné was used to decorate spectacular palace ornaments.

Treating silk cocoons

Gilt finish

A FLOWER MADE FROM A HORN
Objects carved from rhinoceros horn were collectors' items in imperial China. From the Tang dynasty, rhinoceros-horn cups were presented as special gifts to scholars who were successful in their civil service examinations. The Daoists believed that rhinoceros-horn objects possessed magical powers. The rhinoceros-horn cup above is carved in the shape of a lotus blossom, a sacred Daoist flower.

SILK PRODUCTION LINE
The Chinese made silk from at least 3,000 B.C. In imperial China, silk manufacture was a well-organized state industry. Artisans produced large quantities of fine silk cloth in a myriad of rich colours. This luxury fabric was worn by scholars, civil servants, and emperors, and was exported to Asia and Europe along the Silk Road.

Ceremonial conch with silk tassel

The Silk Road

TRADE FLOURISHED under the Mongol, or Yuan dynasty. The Mongol emperors ruled China from 1279 to 1368 and permitted merchants to trade freely throughout their vast empire. They controlled the entire length of the Silk Road, a series of trade routes that ran from northern China across Asia. International trade thrived because caravans could travel without danger. Chinese merchants amassed large fortunes by exporting luxury goods such as silk, spices, teas, porcelain, and lacquer ware. At home in China, the Mongols removed the usual restraints placed upon merchants. Traditionally, merchants were excluded from civil service jobs and were subject to heavy taxes. But for most of their rule, the Mongols ignored the opinions of Chinese officials and the social position of merchants temporarily improved.

THE MONGOL CONQUEST
The Mongols came from north of the Great Wall. They were herdsmen who had expert cavalry skills, which made their army virtually unbeatable. After years of fighting, Genghiz Khan (1167–1227) conquered China. By 1279, the empire was under complete Mongol control. Genghiz Khan's grandson, Kubilai Khan, ruled almost the whole of East Asia until his death in 1294.

PORCELAIN PERFECTION
This magnificent porcelain jar from the Yuan dynasty is an example of the finely crafted ceramics that were exported to Asia and Europe. The "blue and white" style became widely popular in the Ming dynasty, which succeeded the Yuan.

THE LAND OF SILK
The Silk Road took its name from China's most successful export commodity – silk. From the early empire onwards, the Chinese exported fine silk cloth to Asia and Europe. The Romans knew China as Serica, which means "Land of Silk". The secret of silk-making was eventually smuggled out of China, but the Chinese remained the major exporters of silk to Europe until the 19th century.

"Blue and white" jar, 14th century

Knife-shaped bronze coin, c. 500 B.C.

Hole allowed coin to be threaded on a string

A standard round coin introduced by the First Emperor

Butterfly

Peony

Silver pieces, used as money throughout the Chinese empire

Money shaped like a shoe

MAKING MONEY
In ancient times, travelling merchants used silver money shaped like knives or spades. The First Emperor introduced round bronze coins, known as *cash*. They remained in use for over 2,000 years. Paper money first appeared in the 11th century and was widely used in the Yuan dynasty.

Clipped coin

Silver ingot

Standard-sized bolts of silk cloth were used as money between the Han and Tang dynasties

Camels formed long
caravans that
travelled along
the Silk Road

MARCO POLO
During the Yuan dynasty the Khans kept the
peace along the Silk Road, which allowed
foreigners to make the treacherous journey from
Europe to China. Marco Polo (1254–1324) was a
Venetian merchant who travelled to China, then
known in Europe as Cathay, in the 13th century.
He became a favourite of Kubilai Khan and
served as an esteemed official in his civil service
for nearly 20 years. After his return to Italy,
Marco Polo wrote his famous *Travels*. This book
gave Europe its first glimpse of the fabulous
wealth and culture of the Chinese empire.

Saddle

Water bottle

Kubilai Khan with
his horsemen

THE LONGEST JOURNEY
The Silk Road wound its way
across the dry, barren lands that
linked the oasis-cities of central
Asia. Camels were the only beasts
of burden that could survive these
harsh conditions. They carried
only luxury goods because
transport was expensive
and difficult.

THE GREAT KHAN
Kubilai Khan's reign (1216–94) in China
was at the highest point of Mongol power.
The Mongol empire stretched from Asia
to Europe, although expeditions sent
to conquer Japan and Java failed.
Kubilai Khan established a
glittering capital at Kanbula,
which is present-day
Beijing. However, after the
Great Khan died, the
Mongol emperors
struggled to maintain
control over China. In
1368, the Chinese Ming
dynasty succeeded in
driving the Mongols
back into Mongolia.

Ceramic Bactrian
camel, Tang dynasty

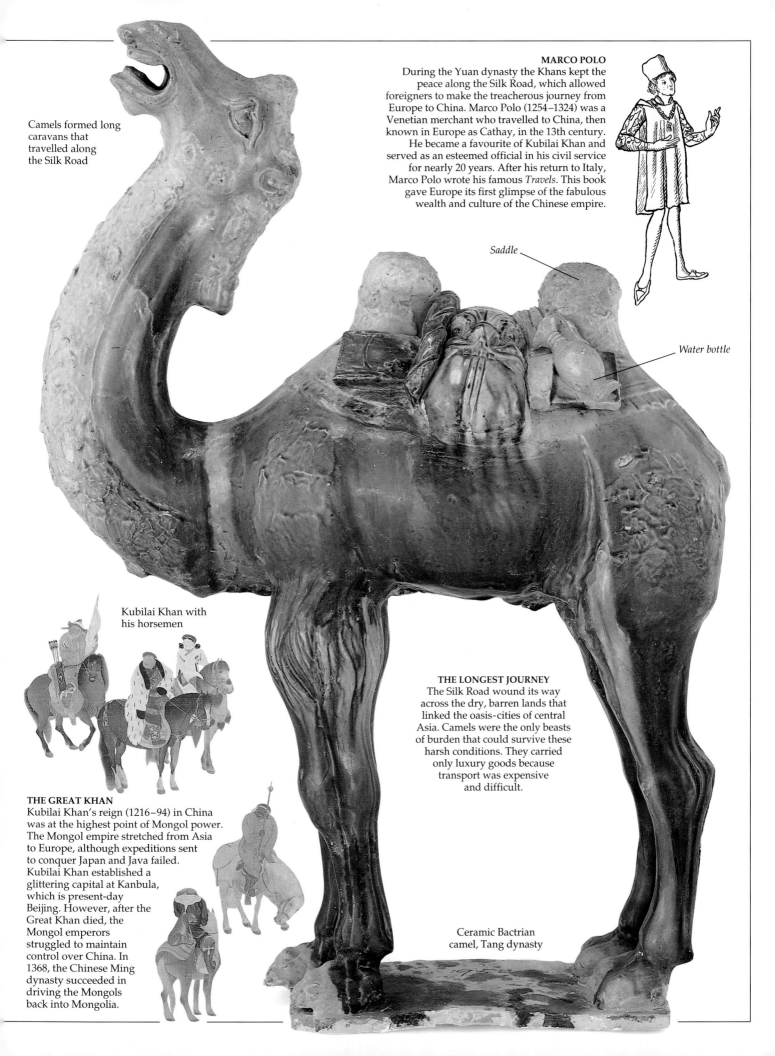

Great ocean voyages

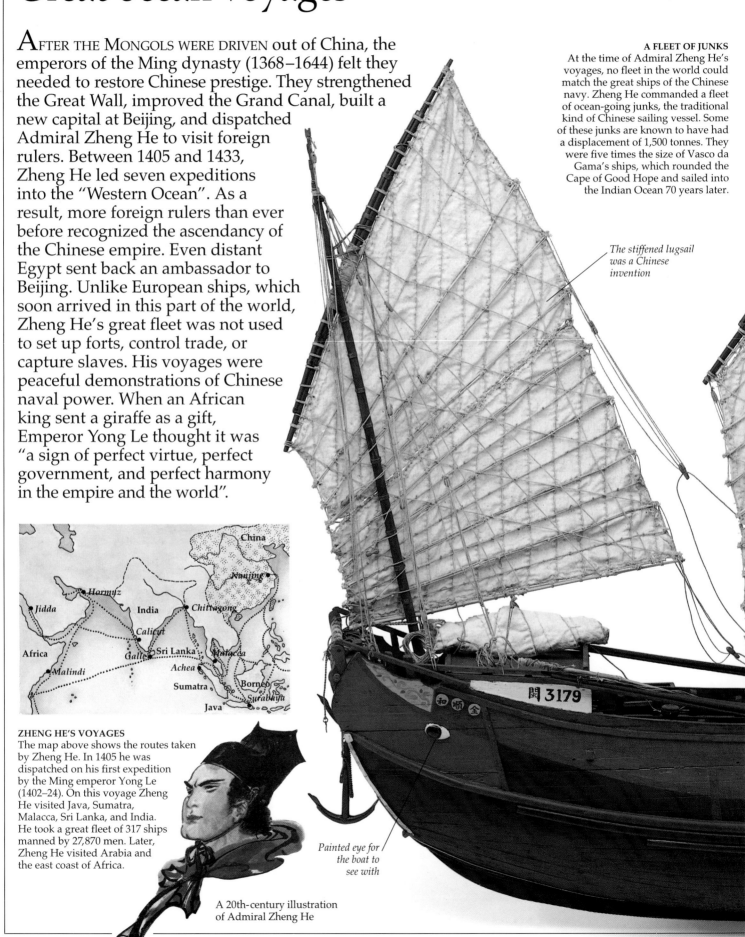

AFTER THE MONGOLS WERE DRIVEN out of China, the emperors of the Ming dynasty (1368–1644) felt they needed to restore Chinese prestige. They strengthened the Great Wall, improved the Grand Canal, built a new capital at Beijing, and dispatched Admiral Zheng He to visit foreign rulers. Between 1405 and 1433, Zheng He led seven expeditions into the "Western Ocean". As a result, more foreign rulers than ever before recognized the ascendancy of the Chinese empire. Even distant Egypt sent back an ambassador to Beijing. Unlike European ships, which soon arrived in this part of the world, Zheng He's great fleet was not used to set up forts, control trade, or capture slaves. His voyages were peaceful demonstrations of Chinese naval power. When an African king sent a giraffe as a gift, Emperor Yong Le thought it was "a sign of perfect virtue, perfect government, and perfect harmony in the empire and the world".

A FLEET OF JUNKS
At the time of Admiral Zheng He's voyages, no fleet in the world could match the great ships of the Chinese navy. Zheng He commanded a fleet of ocean-going junks, the traditional kind of Chinese sailing vessel. Some of these junks are known to have had a displacement of 1,500 tonnes. They were five times the size of Vasco da Gama's ships, which rounded the Cape of Good Hope and sailed into the Indian Ocean 70 years later.

The stiffened lugsail was a Chinese invention

ZHENG HE'S VOYAGES
The map above shows the routes taken by Zheng He. In 1405 he was dispatched on his first expedition by the Ming emperor Yong Le (1402–24). On this voyage Zheng He visited Java, Sumatra, Malacca, Sri Lanka, and India. He took a great fleet of 317 ships manned by 27,870 men. Later, Zheng He visited Arabia and the east coast of Africa.

Painted eye for the boat to see with

A 20th-century illustration of Admiral Zheng He

Bamboo battens stiffen the sail and make it easier to roll up in high winds

Star-chart for the journey between Sumatra and Sri Lanka

Combined compass and sundial

NAVIGATING AT SEA
The Chinese invented the magnetic compass and the star-chart, which were vital aids to navigation. By using these inventions, Zheng He could plot courses straight across the ocean instead of hugging the coastline and risking shipwreck.

Mizzen mast

Rudder

Model of a traditional Chinese junk

The end of the empire

DURING THE LAST 250 YEARS of the Chinese empire, the throne was occupied by the Manchus, a non-Chinese people from north of the Great Wall. China prospered for the first 150 years of the Manchu, or Qing dynasty (1644–1911). The emperors Kangxi (1662–1722) and Qianlong (1736–95) were enlightened rulers who supported Chinese art and culture and maintained the imperial civil service. However, the Qing emperors feared that change might lead to a Chinese rebellion and they clung to outdated traditions. For the first time, Chinese technology fell behind other countries. Britain, France, Russia, and later Japan began to bully the vulnerable Qing empire in order to gain trade concessions. In 1839 a Chinese official in Canton tried to stop the import of opium, which British ships brought from India to exchange for tea. After a clash, Britain declared war upon China and secured a swift victory. This encouraged other countries to demand trade concessions and awards of territory. The Qing dynasty failed to keep foreign powers at bay, and in 1900 an international force captured Beijing. In 1911, the Chinese overthrew their weakened Manchu rulers and set up a republic. The last Qing emperor, the infant Puyi (1906–67), was forced to step down in 1912, bringing to an end 2,000 years of imperial history.

A WISE RULER
The second Qing emperor, Kangxi, successfully secured Manchu rule in China. He was a wise emperor who respected Chinese culture. Unlike the previous foreign rulers, the Mongols, Kangxi employed Chinese scholars in the civil service. Many Chinese became loyal to the Qing dynasty.

PATRON OF THE ARTS
Kangxi's grandson Qianlong enjoyed a long and prosperous reign. He greatly admired Chinese art, which flourished under his patronage. Qianlong filled the imperial palace with a magnificent collection of paintings and artefacts, such as this beautiful elephant.

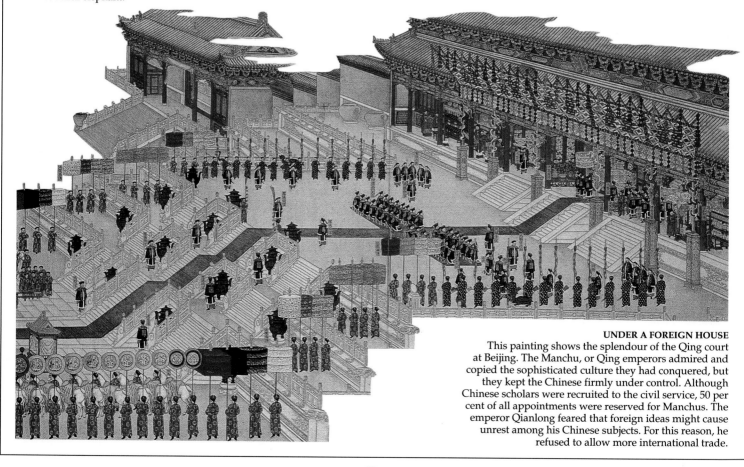

UNDER A FOREIGN HOUSE
This painting shows the splendour of the Qing court at Beijing. The Manchu, or Qing emperors admired and copied the sophisticated culture they had conquered, but they kept the Chinese firmly under control. Although Chinese scholars were recruited to the civil service, 50 per cent of all appointments were reserved for Manchus. The emperor Qianlong feared that foreign ideas might cause unrest among his Chinese subjects. For this reason, he refused to allow more international trade.

Boxer rebels

THE BOXER REBELLION
In 1900, the Boxers, an anti-foreign society in northern China, destroyed imported goods and attacked Christian missions. An international force suppressed the uprising and occupied Beijing. It was the last straw for the Chinese empire.

BY FAIR MEANS OR FOUL
This priceless sceptre was presented to the emperor Qianlong by the French. In the final years of the empire, there was intense rivalry between European powers to become the dominant influence in China. France later seized Vietnam, Laos, and Cambodia, which were ancient Chinese allies.

THE OPIUM WAR
In 1839, commissioner Li Zexu tried to stop the British trading opium at the port of Canton. Britain sent gunboats to support the opium traders, and easily defeated the Chinese, as seen above. The British forced China to open four more ports to foreign trade and to give Hong Kong to Britain. This was the beginning of the end. Soon China had to open 10 more ports and give money and territory to foreign powers such as France and Russia.

DEADLY TRADE
Opium was a drug used in China, but the Qing emperors banned its import when the British began to sell it in vast quantities. The British traded specially grown Indian opium for tea and other prized Chinese exports because the Chinese were uninterested in British goods.

The top of the sceptre is made in the shape of a sacred fungus

Sceptre studded with precious jewels

19th-century opium pipe

Qing good wishes symbols

THE LAST EMPEROR
The last Qing emperor Puyi (1909–1912) was placed on the throne at the age of three. Only three years later, revolutionaries established a republican government and forced him to abdicate. Puyi was allowed to remain in the Forbidden City with his attendants, but conditions worsened until he fled to a Japanese colony in 1924. When the Japanese invaded Manchuria in 1931, Puyi was made emperor of their puppet state, renamed Manzhouguo. After the war, Puyi was imprisoned in China. Freed in 1959, he spent his last years in Beijing.

Index

Acknowledgements

Dorling Kindersley would like to thank:
The staff of the Department of Oriental Antiquities at the British Museum, London, in particular Chris Kirby, Jane Newson and Christine Wilson – with special thanks to Anne Farrer; the British Museum Photographic Department, especially Ivor Kerslake; Marina de Alarçon at the Pitt Rivers Museum, Oxford; Shelagh Vainker at the Ashmolean Museum, Oxford; John Osborne at the Museum of Mankind, London; Monica Mei at the Acumedic Centre, London; the Guanghwa Company Ltd., London; Helena Spiteri for editorial help; Sharon Spencer, Susan St. Louis and Isaac Zamora for design help.
Additional photography by Peter Anderson (62cl, 63cl), Matthew Chattle (50-51t), Andy Crawford (13tr), Philip Dowell (52cl), David Gowers (59c), Chas Howson (23cr, 58bl), Ivor Kerslake (40tl), Dave King (2bl,cr, 40cl), Laurence Pordes (11cr, 19br, 24bl,cr, 25tl,bl), Ranald MacKecknie (54cl), and James Stevenson (23tl, 60-61c)
Maps by Simone End (6tl, 9br, 60bl)
Index by Hilary Bird

Picture credits
a=above, b=below, c=centre, l=left, r=right

Bridgeman Art Library / Bibliotheque Nationale, Paris 16cr, 27tl
By permission of the British Library 24cl
©British Museum 58cl,cr
J. Allan Cash Ltd. 6br
Courtesy Chinese Cultural Embassy 16cl
Comstock / George Gerster 16br, 35tl
Arthur Cotterell 15cl, 22c, 23tr, 24tc, 31cl, 32tr, 44tl,cl, 50br, 53cr, 55tl, 58bl, 62tl
R.V. Dunning FC tl,br, 18c,bc, 31tl, 41bc
ET Archive 34tl / Bibliotheque Nationale, Paris 18tl,39tl,54tl / British Museum FC bl, BC tc, 20tl, 38tl / Freer Gallery of Art 35cr, 36cr / National Palace Museum, Taiwan 42bl / Private Collection 62b / Courtesy Trustees Victoria & Albert Museum 50cr, 57cr
Mary Evans Picture Library 8tr, 12tl, 59tr / T'Ongjen Tschen Kierou King 28bl / Petit Journal BC br, 63tl, Vittorio
Pisari in La Tribuna Illustrata 63br
Robert Harding Picture Library 16tr / Collection of the National Palace Museum,Taipei, Taiwan, Republic of China 59bl
Mansell Collection 26tr, 36tl
National Maritime Museum 63bl
The Needham Research Institute 16bl, 22br
The Nelson-Atkins Museum of Art, Kansas City, Missouri (Purchase: Nelson Trust) 33-1559, 33tr
Photographie Giraudon 40bl
Photostage / Donald Cooper 52tl
Roger-Viollet 60bl
©Science Museum 22bl
Courtesy Trustees of Victoria & Albert Museum 46br, 54cl / Ian Thomas BC tl, 16clb, 21t,bc, 54-5b, 63tr